STEPHEN KING

NEVER FLINCH

A NOVEL

Never Flinch is Stephen King's New Novel!

From master storyteller Stephen King comes an extraordinary new novel with intertwining storylines — one about a killer on a diabolical revenge mission, and another about a vigilante targeting a feminist celebrity speaker — featuring the beloved Holly Gibney and a dynamic new cast of characters.

Unique Exclusives from StephenKingCatalog.com
- First Printing hardcover with Exclusive Glenn Chadbourne wraparound cover
- First Printing hardcover with Exclusive slipcase
- First Printing hardcover Remarqued by Glenn Chadbourne, Slipcased
- Red & Silver Slipcases available separately (see on website)
- Includes an Acid-Free Book cover placed on every book purchased!

You can see all details and order at StephenKingCatalog.com

Pre-order from Stephen KingCatalog.com and you will receive:
- **FREE** bookplate of Stephen King, with art currently featured here by Cortney Skinner with all pre-order purchases!
- **Acid-Free Book Cover** placed on your copy with every purchase.
- **First Printing guaranteed!** We analyze every book to make sure it is As New before sending out.
- **Shipped in a well-packed box for complete Protection.**

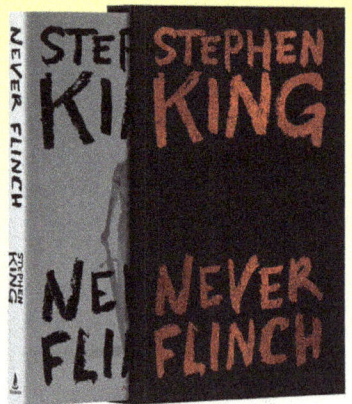

STEPHEN KING

NEVER FLINCH

Visit **StephenKingCatalog.com** to pre-order and read complete details

STEPHEN KING

CALENDAR

-2025-

MEETING STEPHEN KING

Written and Edited by Dave Hinchberger
Cover and Interior Art by Glenn Chadbourne

OVERLOOK CONNECTION PRESS

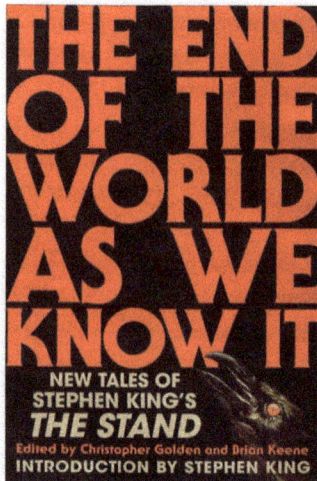

Stars in Their Eyes... Books in Their Arms

I was always a fan of rock music, hell, any music for that matter. If it sounds good, makes you move, *and* feel great… I say turn it up! Earlier in my life I'd managed several record stores and then worked at Polygram Records for a decade. Let me tell you, it was the time of my life. Promoting our bands like KISS, Tears for Fears, RUSH, John Mellencamp, The Scorpions, even Luciano Pavarotti, and I was there when Bon Jovi made it big starting with *Slippery When Wet*. Man, have I got stories (I'm *still* writing that book). Through it all I was reading, reading a lot of Stephen King work. Working with those musicians was fantastic, but it was Stephen King that was the real rock star in my book.

In the late '70's I began with reading Stephen King's *The Shining*, and during my music biz heyday, I created a small mail-order business, The Overlook Connection (get it?), offering unique Stephen King books and items I discovered from King's own newsletter, *Castlerock* (1985-1989). The business grew and became my full-time gig after the music biz. While I was offering his items, Stephen King would tour the country, and the world, when a new release came out. Not for every release mind you, but he travelled quite a bit now and then. This years *Stephen King Calendar: Meeting Stephen King* offers stories and articles from folks who have been to signings, reading events, and appearances from all over the world and throughout the decades. These stories offer a unique insight from folks sharing their moments and who were fortunate enough to see, and even meet, Stephen King. Here's your opportunity to be there with them, and experience these personal moments.

Constant Reader's would travel hundreds, even thousands, of miles, would wait overnight in line, just to get a glimpse of him. Stephen King has always accommodated as many folks as humanly possible, signing and meeting his readers. In 2009 at an Atlanta Barnes & Noble bookstore appearance for *Under the Dome* they featured two ticketed lines for folks to get their book signed. The first line was guaranteed a signature. The second line was a "maybe," in case he couldn't. Well, he signed each-and-every book for both lines. He stuck it out, stayed at his station, and signed each-and-every book handed to him.

Stephen King understands what it means to his readers.

I hope you enjoy this year's *Stephen King Calendar: Meeting Stephen King*. You would also enjoy our *Stephen King Annual, Stephen King On Tour*, as well. It features many articles, reviews, interviews, updates, it also includes the calendar. It's literally twice the size of this edition you hold in your hands with a lot more stories meeting the master that is, Stephen King.

If you have a story to tell about meeting Stephen King or just something unique you'd like to share within the world of Stephen King, drop me a line at **SKAannual@gmail.com**. It would be delightful to hear from you.

Shine on!

– Dave Hinchberger

Stephen King Performs at Hank's Place

by **Dave Hinchberger**

The Ryman Auditorium, June 11th, 2016, 8 p.m.

My wife and I were travelling through North Carolina. We stopped by a Barnes & Noble. Why? It's a bookstore, that's why. This is what we do. It's late in the evening during the week so the store is almost empty. LeeAnn had to go to the other end of the store for something. Within minutes I hear this exclaim of excitement rise to the rafters. I knew it: She ran into a student. I mean we're literally off the beaten path, a couple of states away from home, but they find her. She taught thousands of students at middle school for over thirty years, it's happened many times in many places. She brought Graham over, a working adult now, to meet me. We spoke for a bit. He gave glowing reviews of her time teaching when he was there. I took a photo of them and we left the store but not before checking out at the cashier (I'm sure I found some books in the sale section…).

Stay tuned for the rest… of the story.

The next day she comes up to me and says "you know, Stephen King is going to be in Nashville this summer. I think we should go." She had me at 'King…in Nashville!' Only four hours from Atlanta and the fact that she was already on board with going, this trip

was already happening. This tour was for the *End of Watch* release, no. 3 in the Bill Hodges killer thriller trilogy. With *Mr. Mercedes* (no. 1) previously winning the Edgar Award (Edgar Allen Poe, ya know) from the Mystery Writers of America, I was curious to see what he may have to say about the trilogy now with the final book release. But who are we kidding? His long career of over 60 novels (at that time), original screenplays, short fiction, and all those media adaptations! He could cover any area of his writing and the audience would be at attention, hanging on every sentence, every word.

A day in the life of a King reader trying to get tickets, planning the trip, and travel.

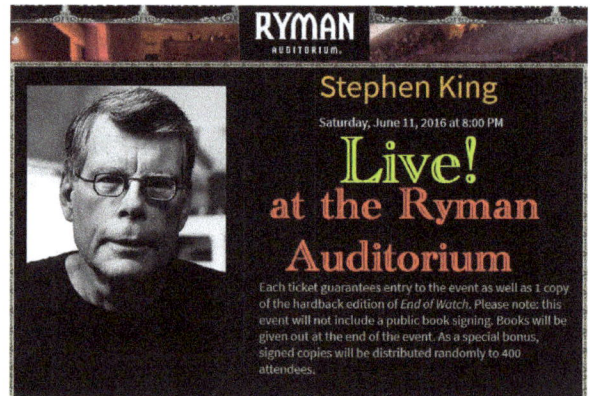

Now the adventure begins. First off we must get tickets! Tickets were about $35 (with fees) and every attendee would receive *End of Watch*. What a bargain! You get the new book and Stephen King in person! To top it off, some copies will be signed! These copies however were given away at random as you left, so there was no guarantee you'd receive one. Only 400 copies were pre-signed at each event on this tour. The Ryman Auditorium can seat 2,362 folks. That's basically a 1 in 5 chance for a signed copy. Here I am, getting ahead of myself. I don't even have tickets yet!

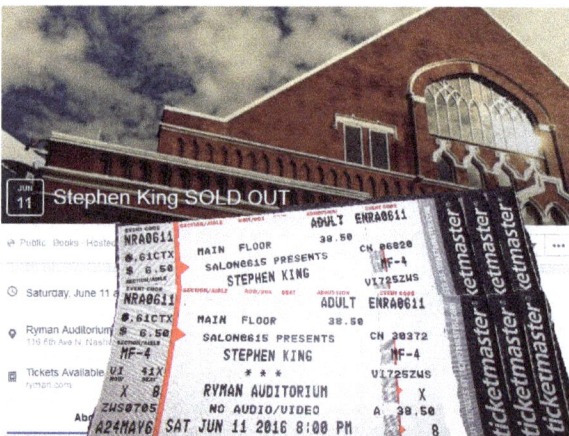

To maximize our opportunity for just acquiring tickets I got in touch with a good friend in Knoxville, Tennessee, Mike Jackson. Mike is often out of town running TV cameras for every Super Bowl, The Masters in Augusta, and sports and music events all around the world (he's won an Emmy for his work!), so he may not be in town. However, he was willing to try and get tickets and we'd figured that between the two of us we could nab at least a couple of pairs.

The morning, 10 am precisely, tickets went on sale, online. The maximum we could get was 8 seats. What the hell, I went for the max. I kept refreshing the website a minute before 10 am until the order button became live, hovering over the keyboard to push enter. There it was! I quickly hit enter… waiting, waiting, the spinning cursor of death kept rotating, and then…it came back with 8 seats! On hold, and I had six minutes to complete my purchase. It was row X.

My son, Ian, had a good question for those uninitiated: he said "Stephen King goes on tour? What does he do?" A valid question. When you hear the word "tour" and at an auditorium, you think bands, not writers. As this row X was staring me in the face I had a quick thought to retry with a lower number of seats and maybe get closer to the "man."

I knew better. I hit purchase, and it completed.My bank account less, but my heart full. Who was I kidding? I've been following this man, this writer, for decades since high school, and he certainly didn't get to where he was because of me and a few others. This man has an immense following! This following was hovering over their keyboards as well. Better to have 8 on X, than 4 of nothing.

I was curious though as this took only about 3 minutes, let's see what else there might be available. 4 tickets: not available. 2 tickets: not available. 1 ticket… there were four single tickets up in the nosebleeds of the Ryman. Basically, it was sold out. Immediately.

I called Stephen King's assistant, the wonderful Marsha Defilippo, to inquire about the tour and told her of my astonishment that the Ryman had sold out, quickly. She said that the Ryman sold out in less than five minutes.

Stephen King
06/12/2016 · 257017

What can I say Driving people out of their minds comes naturally

What can I say? Driving people out of their minds comes naturally to me. Just ask my wife HAHAHAHA.

Almost 2,500 seats… GONE! I checked in with Mike Jackson to see how many seats he attained. Absolutely nothing. He said he couldn't get into the website. Well Mike, no worries, we got 'cha covered!

So now here I was with four extra tickets. As far as I was concerned these were the hottest tickets in Nashville, hell, the surrounding states, as this was the only appearance in the South. I knew what to do. Since the tickets were inexpensive, I mean let's face it, we were able to see Stephen King for basically the price of his latest book. It was an easy decision and the only person I called was Bryan McAllister. You may not know Bryan, but

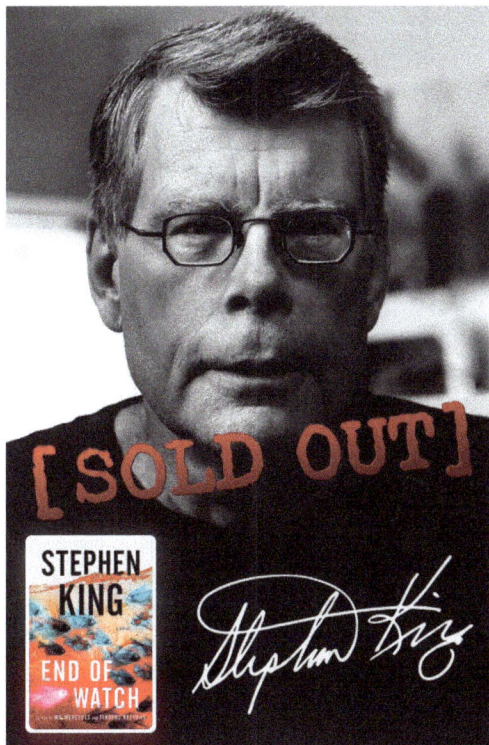

you've been handling his work with every layout of the Stephen King Annuals, and any of our published books from our Overlook Connection Press for years. We've been working together, and friends, for over twenty years. Here was a perfect opportunity to come down from St. Louis (only 4 ½ hours) to Nashville. We would have some great Nashville food, see the sights, and listen to Stephen King in the grand ol' palace they call, The Ryman.

Plans were set. We had Mike Jackson and guest, Bryan and Laura, and LeeAnn and myself. That left us with two last tickets. I had a brilliant idea: Let's auction those off and give the proceeds to Stephen King's Haven Foundation. His charity helped author's and artists in need and gave a grant four times a

year to fortunate recipients for almost two decades. Although the Haven shut down recently, it was truly a gift to those who were in dire straits. To do this I wanted to make sure we went about this the correct way and that the parties involved knew we were auctioning this off for charity. I got in touch with Parnassas Bookstore, who was supporting the event, The Ryman folks, and spoke again with Marsha Defilippo, Stephen King's Senior Assistant. All was a go.

I also thought I'd get in touch with Steve and see if he would promote it via Twitter (remember this is 2016). Here's my conversation with him via e-mail:

During Stephen King's Ryman talk he mentioned that he had Hank Williams old

Email communication with Stephen King

from: **Dave Hinchberger** <overlookcn@aol.com>
to: **Stephen King** <SKing@hisEmail.com>
date: May 16th, 2016, 2:17 PM
subject: **Nashville Tickets up on eBay for the Haven Foundation - 100 damn percent of it :-)**

message: Yo, Steve!
I try to help the Haven Foundation where I can, especially when we have special projects at the stores.
I was able to donate a pair of tickets for your sold out Nashville / Ryman appearance and we put it up tonight on eBay. 100% of the proceeds will head over to the Haven Foundation when it's completed Sunday night, May 22nd.
I've discussed with Marsha and sent her the link, as well as with Parnassas Bookstore there in Nashville, and they have the Ryman on board with this too.
I wanted to share the link with you in case you want to pass it along to the Constant Readers.
Marsha mentioned that this last Haven meeting had one of the highest requests for need ever. I hope this auction will help.
Thank you, again, for all your support over the years. I'm glad, through you, I can offer some support in return to the community.
Hinchy hugs.
Dave
Dave Hinchberger

STEVE's RESPONSE:
Thanks, Dave. You're a good guy.
Steve

DAVE RESPONDS:
Oh... and.. how did you, Mr. "author," get the "Ryman" auditorium during the CMA Music Festival - the biggest country music event of the year?
I hope you bring yer geetar.
Hey, we'll see you from the Ryman cheap seats (but aren't they all? :-)
Have a great tour, Steve.
Dave
Dave Hinchberger

STEVE's RESPONSE:
"Your Cheatin' Heart." Key of G.
God, they better not ask me to play it.
I can't yodel like Hank.
Steve

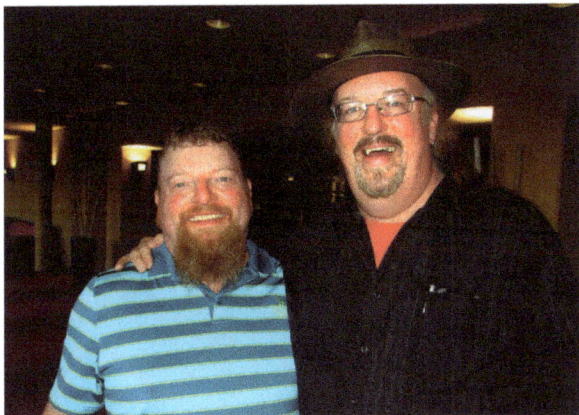
Emmy winner(!) Mike Jackson, and Dave Hinchberger

Constant Readers lined up for Stephen King.

dressing room. Yes, I hear that eerie music in the background too.

The auction went well. We sold the tickets for the auction end price of $405 to a lady in Georgia.

We're all set. Hotel, friends attending with us from all parts, auction tickets delivered, and check sent off to the Haven Foundation. Several months later it's the day of the show. We all meet up at our hotel and head into town to have a wonderful dinner with our group. Next stop: The Ryman.

As we arrive Nashville is hopping! You see it's Country Music week and they close off some of the streets so folks can listen to music, party about town, and the folks are out in droves. The famous Tootsies Orchid Lounge (since 1960) backs up to the Ryman Auditorium and players would get off stage and come out to sneak into the back of Tootsies for a quick drink or play on one of their three stages. When the Overlook Connection crew showed up to the Ryman, the Constant Readers were lined

up around the whole auditorium, amidst the hoopla of Country Music Week. I walked the whole building taking photos of the crowd and was amazed at this sight of King readers waiting patiently among the loud country music coming out of Tootsies, and all the other bars, right next to us. Oh, the dichotomy of it all. It was interesting to see *Carrie*, Stephen King Rules, and *Misery* shirts next to Carrie Underwood posters on the street.

We entered the venue and I told the gang we had to find where they are selling the Hatch Show posters created for the King event (it's the first image you see in this book). I knew we had to get there fast because they only made 200 posters for the event. 200 was a low number, as they don't know King fans. We discovered they were selling them upstairs. We got in the short line and as I was purchasing mine I said "how many are left?" "what you see here." About ten were on the table. Of course, I purchased a second copy. I think Bryan and Mike purchased a couple and they were… gone.

Tootsie's Orchid Lounge, Nashville, Tennessee

Bryan and Laura McAllister, Hatch Show Print shop, Nashville

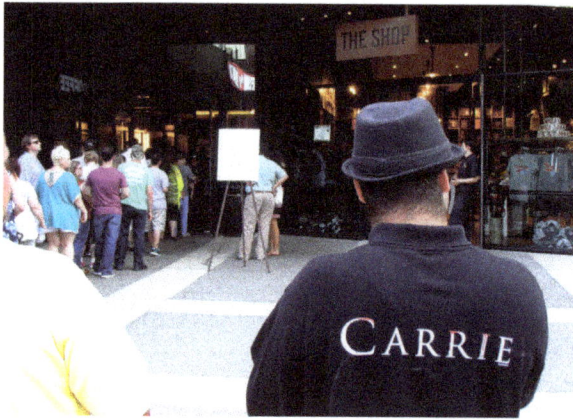

said. "Well, it's all downhill from here. I'm going to talk about writing, but I'm in the Ryman so cut me some slack!"

He told the hilarious story when working on an idea he had for *Gerald's Game*, wherein he asked his 14-year-old son, Joe, to help him work it out by tying him to the bed. This is when his wife Tabby, and Joe's mom, came in and asked what was going on. The crowd roared at this as we could all picture the hilarious scenario. He talked about how he'd practically scared himself writing about the woman in room 217

We met up with our auction winner at our wooden pew, row X. The Ryman was originally a church when built in 1892, thus pews for seating, and stained-glass windows give this grand hall a unique, even grandiose, feel. This lovely lady, all dressed in black, and surprise… was very pregnant. And alone! She said her husband couldn't make it and her mother had to bow out at the last minute. She drove all those hours, pregnant, just to see Stephen King, and of course paid quite a privilege to do so. We made sure to keep her close with our group and we helped her throughout the evening and made sure she received her book, etc. She'll have this story to tell her offspring the rest of your life, "yes, you were there, at the Ryman, with Stephen King on stage."

The evening began with Parnassus Books co-owner, Ann Patchett, who introduced author Donna Tartt, who in turn introduced Stephen King. He entered the stage to a standing ovation with the widest smile on his face. He gave Donna Tartt a hug and then spoke directly to the crowd. "A standing 'O' in the Ryman," he

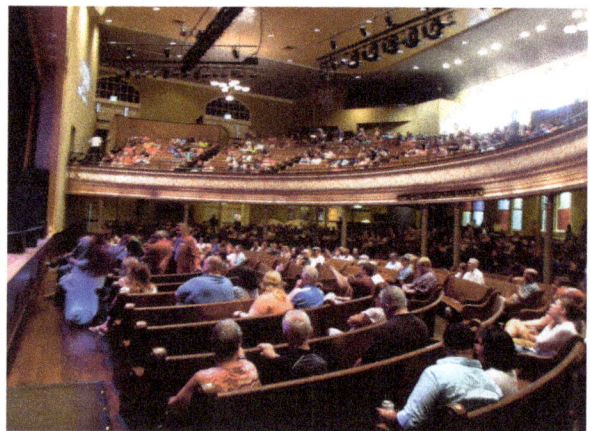

in *The Shining*. He also told us he decided to release *'Salem's Lot* as his second novel, even though he knew it might label him as a horror writer. He mentioned that the original title was Second Coming but Tabby told him it sounded too much like a "sex novel" and that idea was nixed. He also took a moment to inform us that he is working on a novel with son Owen, a novel set around a women's prison in West Virginia, which we now know is *Sleeping Beauties*.

All photos outside and inside, the Ryman Auditorium

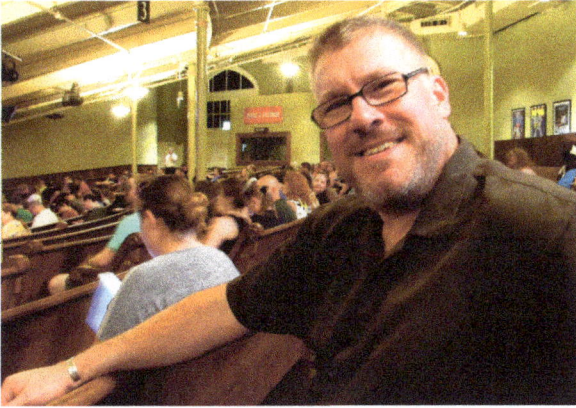
Bryan McAllister on row X, Ryman Auditorium

He talked about Jerry Lee Lewis and what he pulled from his biography. The first time Jerry Lee saw a piano he wrote, "I didn't know what it was but I knew I had to get at it." King said that "comes as close as possible to summarizing what that is, that something that speaks to a person. A guitar, a typewriter, a certain kind of story. For me it was finding a box of my father's paperbacks in the attic. My father left my mother when I was 2, and he left behind many things from his days in the Merchant Marines. What I liked was a box of pulp paperbacks and it contained a collection of H.P. Lovecraft stories called *The Thing From the Tomb*, and I looked at that book and I just knew I had to get at it. Whatever it was awoke in me."

He explained how he thought he became "The King of Horror."

"There was a moment where these two books were sitting on my editor's desk. On one curb I was just Stephen King the adult novelist, and on the other I was Stephen King the horror writer. I said to Bill 'which one of these books do you think I should publish?' Bill said, 'Well, that depends on whether or not you want to be known as a precious novelist, that kind of writer, or go for the big casino and try to grab the brass ring because the vampire novel is a lot better, but he said you'll be known as a horror writer.'" Stephen King said "as long as they will pay me… and then I stopped, I looked down and there was a twenty-dollar bill laying there. I picked up the twenty and I told him let's publish the vampire novel! And that's how I became known as (said in a booming voice) *The King of Horror*."

"What really happened is Boris Karloff died, then Rod Serling died, and then Alfred Hitchcock died, and then somebody up there said 'okay, that's it, you're the Great Pumpkin!'" The crowd then roared in laughter.

During a discussion to an audience member's question, King said: "Writing a novel is like crossing the Atlantic in a row boat. It's tough, and it's not a job for sissies. So, you can't give in, you can't weaken and I think that's pretty good advice for a lot of things."

An audience member asked "what was a good King novel to start with for a first-time reader?"

Stephen King replied: "for 10 or 11 year-olds, *The Girl Who Loved Tom Gordon* or *The Eyes of the Dragon*. What I really like is the outlaw kids who go out on their own, find their own kind of books, and read them under the covers."

The Auction Winner! and Dave Hinchberger

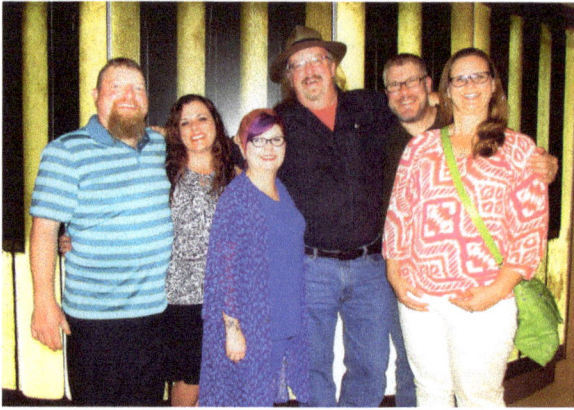
The Overlook Connection crew, Nashville

Dave and Bryan, good old friends in Nashville

Before closing out the night, King remarked, "Everything is happening in Nashville this weekend," he said. "The CMA Fest, Bonnaroo is close by…and look at this place, full of people who read books."

As we left the Ryman we all had to exit out of one set of doors as this is where they were distributing the books. My group was already ahead of me as I stepped back to let some group in front of me that was obviously together. When I got outside the doors there were two groups of people handing out books. The table to the left of me was closer so I took that path. I was handed a copy of *End of Watch* and to my right a lady screamed as she opened her book and saw it was signed. With my book in hand I took a quick peak at the title page… and damn… hot damn!… It was signed! I found my crew and told LeeAnn… she promptly traded her unsigned book… for mine…lol! My wife, such a cut-up that one.

Stephen King told a lot of familiar stories, some expanded, that I've heard over the years at these book events, and I was glad to hear them again, as well as many new tales. He knows how to engage his audience and this reflects how he's able to pull them in on stage, but especially, on the page.

We called it a night and turned in. The next morning we'd checked out of the hotel, and met in the lobby to head out. We were leaving the hotel and we passed the female cashier – went outside to give the valet our ticket and realized I needed a few bucks for his tip. I went back inside to the cashier stand and now there was a young gentleman there. "Can I help you?"

Lo and behold, it was LeeAnn's student, Graham. I said "Graham?" He looked at me and said "Mr. Hinchberger?" I said "yep, and your teacher is right outside, let me get her." I went out and told her "there's someone in here who'd like to see you." She looked at me quizzically but followed me back in. She went wide-eyed when she saw him.

Yes, there were screams and hugs again.

What are the odds?

If I hadn't needed change…

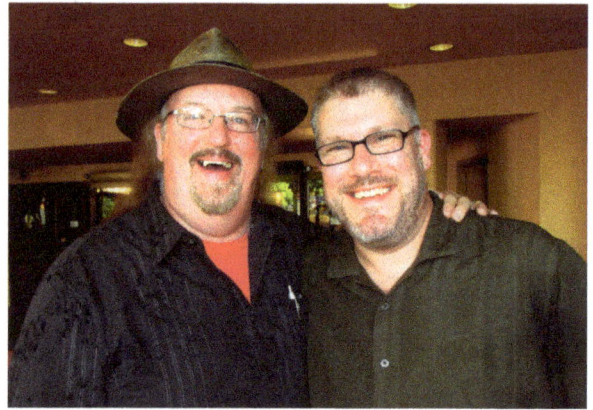

Public Posts

Stephen King
10 hrs

Thanks to everyone who came out tonight to the Ryman in Nashville. We had a good time, didn't we?

3.3K   261 Comments 61 Shares

Like   Comment   Share

Graham and LeeAnn, Nashville

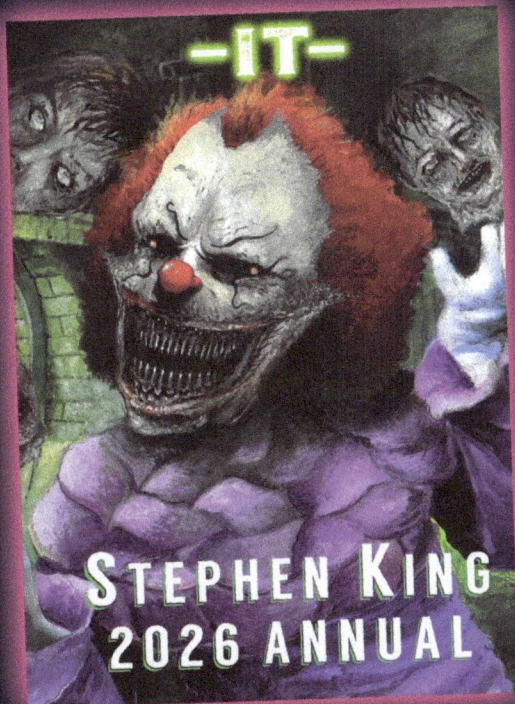

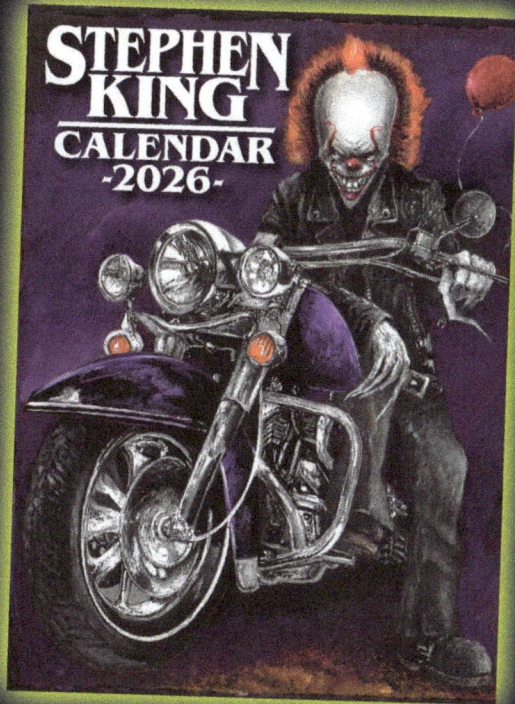

2026 STEPHEN KING ANNUAL: *IT*

The 2026 Annual celebrates Stephen King's novel, *IT*!

The Annual is full color and is 250 pages!

We delve into everything *IT* and Pennywise, the book, the films, merchandise, and everything in-between. Pennywise the clown, a malevolent entity, has become an iconic character the world over. The kids of *IT*, the heroes of this story, are members of The Losers' Club, a group of seven outcast children who are terrorized by Pennywise as *IT* emerges from the sewer.

Expect the usual photos, illustrations, informative articles, interviews, and reviews that are featured in every Stephen King Annual. The Annual also includes the *Stephen King Calendar* with facts, trivia, and art.

THE STEPHEN KING CALENDAR 2026

The 2026 Calendar Features Stephen King's novel, *IT*, All Year Long!

The *Stephen King Calendar* is also in color with 136 pages!

It's overflowing with trivia, facts, illustrations, photos, and with original border art by Glenn Chadbourne throughout the year. The *Stephen King Calendar* is now available separately for those that would like a calendar to use all year long!

If you're familiar with our Stephen King Calendars, then you know what to expect, and they are featured in full-color!

Both the ANNUAL and CALENDAR feature original cover and interior art by Glenn Chadbourne, this year featuring images from *IT* and Pennywise throughout.

Both are available for pre-order at **StephenKingCatalog.com**

Written and Edited by Dave Hinchberger
Also features Artwork by Glenn Chadbourne

Coming Fall 2025

Published by
Overlook Connection Press

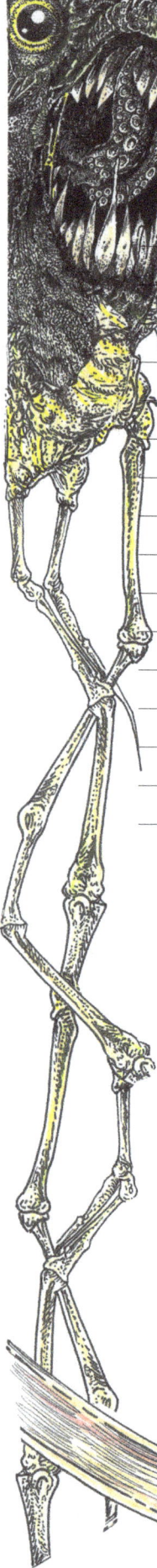

DECEMBER

23 MONDAY

24 TUESDAY
Christmas Eve

25 WEDNESDAY
Christmas Day

'SALEM'S LOT – 2024 FILM – A REVIEW

'Salem's Lot is Glenn's favorite novel by Stephen King. With that in mind I asked if he'd like to impart a few words about the latest movie version, released to the US in October 2024 on MAX, and he obliged us. Take it away Mr. Chadbourne!

Here's my review of *'Salem's Lot.* If you're looking for a blow-by-blow line-by-line adaption, watch the old mini-series (which holds up well in creepy splendor). Better still, give the book a fresh read. That said, I liked it. It veers around a bit, but the basic material's in there —with a bite. The thing I liked most was they made it a period piece set in the mid-seventies (which of course was when the book was written) and they NAILED IT. Rural Maine was a very different place then than it is now. I should know, I've lived here all my life. Beer cans and litter of all kinds lined roadsides. There were open air town dumps that continually smouldered. Everyone smoked. You'd ride seven or so kids packed into the backs of pickup trucks. No bike helmets, seat belts etc. There were plenty of drugs but none that would kill you in a hurry. In short, you could smell mid seventies Maine. The film did a great job capturing the vibe/atmosphere. Great soundtrack too. For me it was a fun movie and I was satisfied.

When it comes to vampire screen offerings there seem to be a few regularly used formulas. There's the romantic formula, where the main vamp is a tragic sympathetic character, as in 'this really isn't his or her fault, this fate was leveled in a cursed fashion the he or she is forced to endure. Think of the *Twilight* sagas, with gooshy golden sheened glowing teenage angst

New Stephen King Cover Series No. 3, *'Salem's Lot.* Art by Glenn Chadbourne

DECEMBER

26 THURSDAY

Hanukkah (1st day)
Kwanzaa

27 FRIDAY

28 SATURDAY

29 SUNDAY

New Year's Eve

love triangles. These are great if you're a brooding goth kid picnicking in boneyards. Actually, Gary Oldman's role as Drac' came across as a sympathetic character in the film's end. Drac' of course has as many interpretations as the many actors who've played him through the years. I'm a Christopher Lee man m'self. Then you have the dour, broody, Anne Rice versions in gothic splendor, richly outfitted with inner searching self-loathing complex characters. These too would find goth kids happily picnicking in the boneyard. Of these, both the old Brad Pitt/Tom Cruise film version as well as the recent series are pretty swell, in my humble op'. There are inventive versions of vamp culture that pop up every so often. The original *Fright Night* is a fun ride with a fresh feel for its time that I really enjoyed. *Near Dark* is a masterpiece in my view, with nasty outlaw vamps cruising around and sucking up the southwest states. Like *'Salem's Lot* Maine in the mid-seventies you could smell this outfit coming. If you want downright brutal scary as fuck vampires I'd have to hand that title to the *30 Days of Night* flick. That breathed fresh fear into the genre. Playing the mood in a pitch perfect key I'd hand it to the cable version of *Chapelwaite*, which delivers (I think) the perfect vibe of slow creeping dread brilliantly. It's played straight, and the vamps in that universe are believable and hideous. This is among the greatest film adaptations of SK's work (again in my humble op'). There are many other lesser-known films/ tv series, etc., but these are the ones that pop into my noggin. I'd put the new Lot version more in the 'fun' category. As I said, I liked it, but if you're a purist, watch Tobe Hooper's *'Salem's Lot* mini-series from the 70's. In defense of the new film, they only had a couple hours to play with, and you can't jam all the intricate goings-on of the story sandwiched into that. In the end, vamps have always been with us and always will be. They suck, and we like to watch them do it.

— Glenn Chadbourne, October 2024

'Salem's Lot New King cover
available at
StephenKingCatalog.com

DECEMBER

30 MONDAY

31 TUESDAY
New Year's Eve

1 WEDNESDAY
New Year's Day

CHRISTINE. . . SAVES!

"...and suddenly there were arms around her, crushing, and a pair of hard hands were clasped together in a knot just below her breasts, in the hollow of her solar plexus. And suddenly one thumb popped up, the thumb of a hitchhiker signaling for a ride, only the thumb drove painfully into her breastbone. At the same time the grip of the. arms tightened brutally. She felt caught (Ohhhhhhh you're breaking my RIBS) in a gigantic bearhug. Her whole diaphragm seemed to heave, and something flew out of her mouth with the force of a projectile. It landed in the snow: a wet chunk of bun and meat." — Stephen King, *Christine*

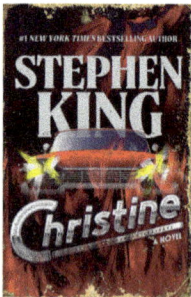

Scribner trade paperback, 2024

My story regarding the King of horror is slightly different to the meet and greets or tour sightings, in fact for all I know he was three thousand miles away, furiously working on his next book when his work helped to save my life.

I was seven years old, that day in 1992 in fact as it was on my birthday that I almost died.

I was in the back of my parent's car heading to Thorpe Park (a UK theme park) to celebrate my birthday, happily sucking on a boiled sweet which suddenly slipped down my throat and became lodged. I remember frantically waving for my parents attention, only able to make guttural noises, when my mum noticed and screamed for my dad to pull over.

JANUARY

2 THURSDAY

3 FRIDAY

4 SATURDAY

5 SUNDAY

There we were, on the side of the motorway...I was yanked from the car and slammed on the back to no avail. My Dad hung me upside down and smacked my back harder but still the sweet was lodged.

I was becoming light headed and starved for air, the passing cars becoming a distant whisper when all of a sudden my lower chest was compressed and a gush of air dislodged the sweet, which went flying like a missile into the bushes

I greedily gulped in fresh air (as fresh as motorway air can be anyway) and from that moment forward never ate one of those sweets again.

"I remember it like it was yesterday; I'd not long since read *Christine* and after I felt Sean tapping my shoulder in the car I turned and realised he was choking, just like Leigh in the book. I remembered how the Heimlich manoeuvre was described so vividly and, after attempts to dislodge the sweet with hits to the back over his Dad's knee failed...I recalled exactly how the hitchhiker saved Leigh and I told his Dad to bring Sean to me. I got my arms around him, balled my fists together and squeezed hard just beneath the ribs...needless to say, it worked!"

— Rachael Chard, Sean's mum.

Whilst it was my Mum (who gets vast majority of credit for saving my life that day) that applied the Heimlich manoeuvre, it was the description of the manoeuvre from *Christine*, which she had recently been reading, that taught her the procedure, During the scene where the hitchhiker saves Leigh Cabot's life and therefore, my life was saved that day in part thanks to Stephen King! Thanks Steve!!

— Sean Chard, Constant Reader since 1995, England

JANUARY

6 MONDAY   **7** TUESDAY   **8** WEDNESDAY

WHO'S ZOOMIN' WHO?

2022 Cheltenham Literacy Festival

In the current age of digital technology you can communicate with the world, face-to-face, just by sitting in front of your laptop. With Zoom, Facebook, etc. facilitating these almost-in-person moments, Stephen King has taken advantage of this to appear for several different interviews and appearances, especially during the years of Covid when traveling was severely restricted.

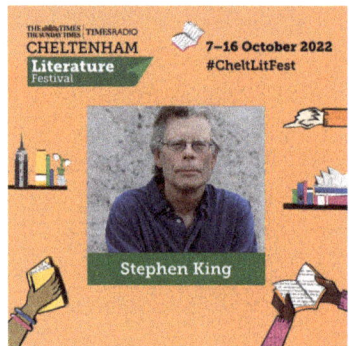

One such appearance was at the Cheltenham Literacy Festival on October 8th, 2022 to celebrate and accept his *Sunday Times* Award for Literary Excellence. This remote appearance was from his home to the private event held at the Cheltenham Town Hall at the Baillie Gifford Stage, and only available for those that could attend the venue in person. Tickets were £17 ($22 US) and the 900-seat venue sold out immediately. He was interviewed by BBC Radio 4 journalist Mark Lawson as King appeared on stage via a large video screen.

JANUARY

9 THURSDAY   **10** FRIDAY   **11** SATURDAY

12 SUNDAY

James Mortimer attended this event and had this to say about attending:

"I virtually met Stephen King (along with a sold-out audience) when he won a *Sunday Times* literacy award at the 2022 Cheltenham Literacy Festival in the UK. Even though he appeared on zoom he had the audience captivated. He discussed his new book, *Fairy Tale*, and told some really, funny tales.

Cheltenham Town Hall at the Baillie Gifford Stage

He did take questions from the audience. The host, Mark Lawson, asked King some pre-prepared questions and King would answer them and crack jokes in real time through the video link. After that the audience could post questions on an online site, which the host read out to ask King. King took quite a few questions from the audience which was fun to experience!

One question had an audience member asking why he hates dogs as they always end up dead in his books! Of course, he mentioned Mollie, "the thing of evil", to remind us he doesn't really hate dogs but uses them to create an emotional hold on the reader.

It was such an honour to be in an audience that where he got to communicate and chat with us digitally. and I am so glad I got the opportunity! Hopefully sometime soon he will come to the UK and I will be privileged enough to meet him."

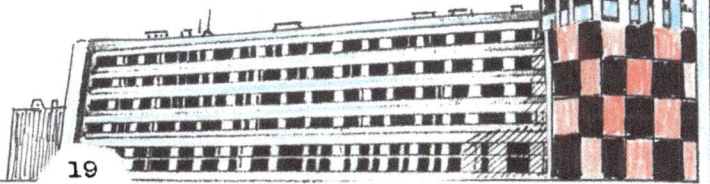

JANUARY

13 MONDAY

14 TUESDAY

15 WEDNESDAY

ENCOUNTERS

My first encounter with Stephen King was way, way, way back in the early '80s when he was set to appear at a middle school library in Truth or Consequences, New Mexico. He was hosting a screening of *Cujo* and signing books to raise funds for the library, where one of his friends worked. Living in El Paso, I eagerly hopped on my motorcycle and rode the 90-minute trek over Trans Mountain Road to meet my favorite author. I even still have the ticket!

The event was fantastic. After the screening, King took to the podium in the school gymnasium, sharing insights about the movie and reminding us with a chuckle, "No matter what the movie says... we all know the kid really dies..." He also touched on Kubrick's *The Shining*, but I'll spare you his colorful commentary on that for the sake of any family-friendly readers.

Post-event, They set up King at the Geronimo Springs Museum for the signing. The line was huge, far exceeding the crowd at the speaking event. After a couple of hours, I found myself near the front door, chatting with folks in line. Suddenly, a tall, lanky gentleman strode past—it was Stephen King himself. He addressed the entire crowd, apologizing for having to close down the line in order to make it to the airport for a late-night flight. Luckily, I was close enough to the door to allow him to usher me in with a few others. I got a photo of him signing someone else's book and had my copy of *Pet Sematary* signed. It was a fantastic night, and I became an even bigger fan, impressed by his personal touch in addressing the crowd directly, and not sending out an assistant to make the announcement.

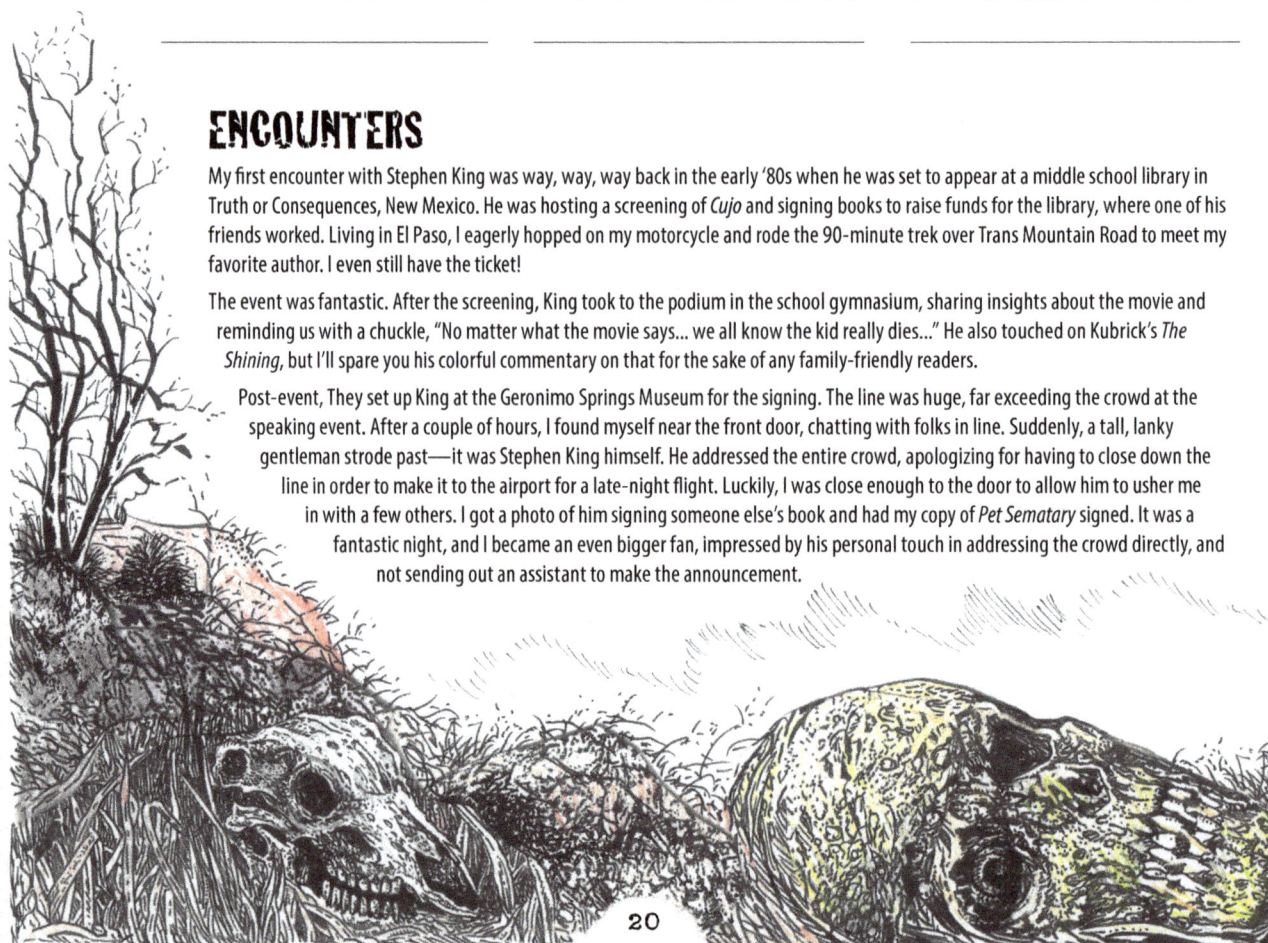

16 THURSDAY

17 FRIDAY

18 SATURDAY

_____
_____
_____
_____
_____
_____
_____
_____
_____
_____
_____
_____
_____
_____
_____
_____

19 SUNDAY

No 980

The Friends of the Truth or Consequences Library
invite you to hear

STEPHEN KING

Saturday, November 19, 1983, at 7:00 p.m.
Truth or Consequences Middle School, 4th & Grape
DONATION: $2.00   DONATION: $4.00
Friends of the Library   Non-members
Senior Citizens
Students

Reception to follow at Geronimo Springs Museum
where an assortment of mr. King's books will
be on sale, including his newest:
"Pet Sematary"

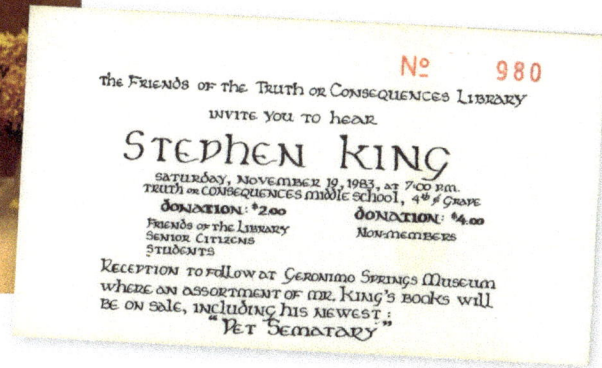

Photo and ticket, Truth or Consequences New Mexico from
Michael Edwards collection, 1983

20 MONDAY
Inauguration Day
Martin Luther King Jr. Day

21 TUESDAY

22 WEDNESDAY

STEPHEN KING DRIVE-IN

Fast forward to 1984: I had moved to Dallas and heard Stephen King would be attending the Joe Bob Briggs Drive-In Movie Festival at the Inwood Theater. No way was I missing that. I went, armed with the framed photo I'd taken of him the previous year, which I had blown up to movie poster size of 20x30. Along with the photo, I brought my original Land of Enchantment first edition of *Cycle of the Werewolf*. This was pre-iPhone, so no selfies, but I snapped quite a few photos from the event. Again, I was impressed as rather than showing up in a limo or with a driver, King drove up in a small rental car… parked and walked up to greet fans wearing a *Christine* t-shirt.

When I had the chance to talk to him, he loved the huge photo and signed it, "For Mike, Beast Wishes, Big Steve King" and then dated it. The autograph has faded over the years, but thankfully it's still visible. When I handed him my *Cycle of the Werewolf* book, he happily signed it, and Tabitha King, who was hanging out with him at the table, asked if she could sign it too. Of course, I said yes! So, she added her signature to it.

It was an amazing weekend, the best part being the opportunity for a few fans to have breakfast with Stephen King at the small restaurant that was attached to the Inwood Theater. Here's the catch: all you had to do was stay awake all night through an "Iron Man Marathon" of bloody movies and we hung out for a bit the following morning. All in all, it was an incredible experience for a Stephen King fan, but admittedly I still hold out hope for an opportunity to meet him just one more time!!

JANUARY

23 THURSDAY

_____
_____
_____
_____
_____
_____
_____
_____
_____
_____
_____
_____
_____
_____

24 FRIDAY

_____
_____
_____
_____
_____
_____
_____
_____
_____
_____
_____
_____
_____
_____

25 SATURDAY

_____
_____
_____
_____
_____
_____
_____

26 SUNDAY

_____
_____
_____
_____
_____
_____
_____

On a side note, just a couple of years before his passing, I showed the _Cycle of the Werewolf_ book to Berni Wrightson, who signed both it and my first edition _Creepshow book_. Wrightson was truly a class act.

– Michael Edwards
Anderson Farms / Terror in the Corn
terrorinthecorn.com

Stephen King signing for fans
1984 Inwood Theater Dallas

John Bloom (aka Joe Bob Briggs)
and Stephen King

Photos: 1984 Michael Edwards

1984 - Joe Bob Briggs Drive In Movie Festival

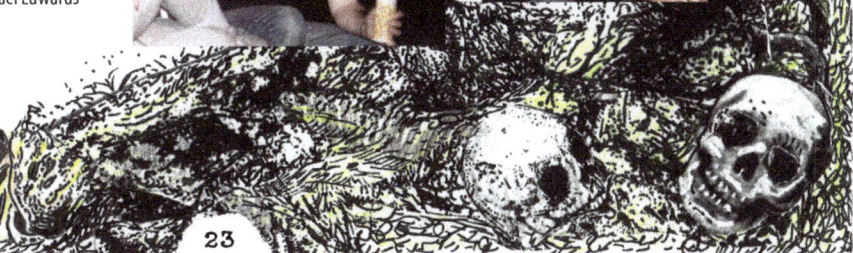

JANUARY

27 MONDAY

28 TUESDAY

29 WEDNESDAY
Lunar New Year

SIX-PACK TO GO

In 1981, the seventh World Fantasy Convention was held at the Claremont Hotel in Berkeley, California. Among the guests was Stephen King, who took part in several panels and was a World Fantasy Award nominee for Best Novel, for *The Mist*. He didn't win (that one went to Gene Wolfe, who won in that category again in 2007, the year I was a judge), but *Dark Forces*, Kirby McCauley's anthology *Dark Forces*, in which *The Mist* had appeared, did win for Best Anthology or Collection. So King shared in that reflected glory, at least.

King was already a literary celebrity, of course, and typically drew a crowd wherever he was in the hotel. At one point I was sitting in the hotel bar (then, as now, the place for socializing at WFC) when King entered. Knowing he couldn't sit at the bar and have a drink without crowds gathering, he bought a six-pack of bottled beer from the bartender and started back toward his room.

But the crowd had already arrived, and it surrounded him as he left the bar, barking compliments and questions in about equal measure.

King conversed with them for ten or fifteen minutes, as his cold beer warmed. After a while, I left the bar to visit the adjacent men's room, and while I washed my hands, King came in—followed by a fan. "Mr. King!" the fan said. "I just have one question!" "I just have to take a piss," King growled.

Presumably he did so. I was out of the restroom by then, and so was the chastised fan.

A couple minutes later, I was on my way to the staircase to meet someone, and King came out of the restroom, headed for the same staircase. But again, he was waylaid; this time by a mature, nicely dressed woman. I don't know if he knew her, but he paused when she said, "Mr. King, may I introduce you to someone?"

WFC 1981 Cover art
1981 by Edina and Orvy Junds

24

JANUARY

30 THURSDAY

31 FRIDAY

1 SATURDAY

2 SUNDAY
Groundhog Day

I didn't hear his response, but by now I was curious. The only other person in the immediate vicinity was a young woman sitting by herself on a settee with a red-tipped, white cane leaning beside her. I stayed put.

The woman led King straight to her. "Christine," she said, "This is Mr. King. Mr. King, this is Christine. She's been wanting to meet you."

I watched the smile spread across King's face. If you've seen it, you know the one I'm talking about: genuine enthusiasm combined with a hint of mischievousness.

"Christine?" said he, shaking her proffered hand. "I have to tell you about the book I'm working on."

With that, he sat beside her and started describing his work-in-progress.

Twenty or thirty minutes later, I passed by again. Stephen King and Christine were still sitting there, deep in conversation, his by now room-temperature six-pack forgotten at his feet.

Whenever someone asks me what Stephen King is like, I tell that story. It sums him up nicely, I believe.

— Jeffrey J. Mariotte

WFC 1981 Back cover art
1981 by Alfredo P. Alcala

FEBRUARY

3 MONDAY   **4** TUESDAY   **5** WEDNESDAY

VANDAL . . . KING?

One of the world's most famous authors, Stephen King, was mistaken for a vandal in an Alice Springs bookstore on Tuesday.

Dymocks store manager Bev Ellis says a customer saw the horror novelist walk into the store.

Once inside, King found copies of his books and began signing them.

"As the owner of a bookshop, when you see someone writing in one of your books you get a bit toey (anxious)" Ms. Ellis said.

"So, we immediately ran to the books and low-and-behold here was the signature in several books.

"We sort of spun around on our heels, [saying] 'where did he go, where did he go'."

Ms. Ellis says she saw the author standing in the fruit and veg section of the supermarket across the road.

"So, I went over and introduced myself ... He was lovely, very nice, charming," she said.

Ms. Ellis says she asked him if he was staying long in Alice Springs and he just smiled.

FEBRUARY

Ms. Ellis also said she assumed the author was on a holiday and had come into the shop to check to see that *Lisey's Story*, his most recent book, had been stocked.

"[Then I said], well if we knew you were coming we would have baked a cake."

"He introduced me to his friends and we had a talk and then I said 'Well I'll leave you to the tomatoes.'"

Asked if it was the first time an author had simply come in a started signing, Ms. Ellis replied: "They don't normally just open the books and go for it."

But she said the high-profile writer was polite and well spoken.

King signed six books in total.

The customer that mistook the author for a vandal bought one. Ms. Ellis plans to give the remaining five copies to community groups who can auction them off to raise funds.

King's rep in Sydney confirmed that they did not know the author was currently in Australia. August, 2007.

The bookstore, Dymocks Alice Springs, owned by Bev Ellis and her husband since 1993, closed its doors in 2013 after a twenty-year run in the business.

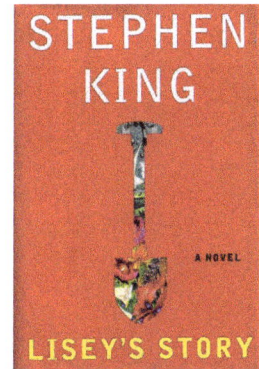

Lisey's Story, Scribner 2006

This story created from combined news reports at abc.net.au and www.brisbanetimes.com.au

FEBRUARY

HITTING ROCK BOTTOM WRITING

In the "First Foreword" to Stephen King's *On Writing* he discusses how The Rock Bottom Remainders was to be a one-time event: "The group was intended as a one-shot deal—we would play two shows at the American Booksellers Convention, get a few laughs, recapture our misspent youth for three or four hours, then go our separate ways." And then he mentions how it obviously didn't happen that way as "the group never quite broke up." So then as the group continued to play and in 1993 went on tour across the country they found themselves in Miami Beach eating Chinese food before a show. Stephen King and Amy Tan were having a discussion, about the one question that was never asked during the Q-and-A following almost every writer's talk. He said Amy Tan was thinking it over when she finally said "No one ever asks about the language." Something obviously clicked because King said he owed "an immense dept of gratitude" for her response. He had been thinking of writing a book about writing but didn't trust his own "motivations," thinking since he'd sold so many books he might have something "worthwhile to say about

On Writing, Scribner 2020

28

FEBRUARY

13 THURSDAY

_____
_____
_____
_____
_____
_____
_____
_____
_____
_____
_____
_____
_____
_____
_____
_____

14 FRIDAY

Valentine's Day

_____
_____
_____
_____
_____
_____
_____
_____
_____
_____
_____
_____
_____
_____
_____
_____

15 SATURDAY

_____
_____
_____
_____
_____
_____
_____

16 SUNDAY

_____
_____
_____
_____
_____

writing." But just because he sold a lot of books he'd thought he'd better have a better reason than just being "successful." His reference to Colonel Sanders selling a lot of Fried Chicken doesn't mean folks want to hear how he made it. That's pure Stephen King right there.

Amy Tan's response, that nobody asks about the language gave Stephen King the go ahead to begin the book *On Writing*. He said "that no one ever asks (them) about the language." They ask "the DeLillos and the Updikes… but they don't ask popular novelists. Yes many of us proles also care about the language…" He dedicated the book to Amy Tan because she "told me in a very simple and direct way that it was okay to write it." *On Writing* was born while the Rock Bottom Remainders were on tour. Inspiration hits when it hits… over a meal before a show.

Photo: Shane Leonard

FEBRUARY

17 MONDAY
President's Day

18 TUESDAY

19 WEDNESDAY

KING BY CANDLELIGHT

Our very own "Extreme King" co-author, Diana Petroff, discovered a signed copy of *Insomnia* for sale, on Facebook Marketplace. As she contacted the seller she inquired about its provenance. The seller had won the chance to buy a signed copy in a raffle, while Stephen King read a chapter from *Insomnia* to a small crowd... by candlelight.

Photo:
Michael Edwards,
1984

Now this is a first: I had never heard of Stephen King reading by candlelight to an audience.

I got in touch with the seller because now I had questions. She said "I had to buy a raffle ticket to win the chance to buy the book. That night, he read from *Insomnia* for those of

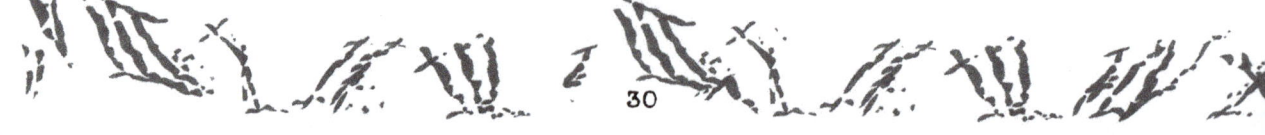

FEBRUARY

20 THURSDAY   **21** FRIDAY   **22** SATURDAY

23 SUNDAY

us that won, in a room in Legislative Plaza in Nashville. It was soooo creepy. he had one big blood red candle for light. There were about thirty people in the audience. I was in the front row so I didn't see exactly how many came in behind us, you know with just candlelight… one candle. It was called the War Memorial Auditorium. He had a tall black candleholder with a large red pillar candle. He read from a podium and I think he had a light over the book so he could read. It was from *Insomnia* but I have no idea which part. We all knew what was going to happen, and being scared was a crazy thought….after all, it's just a book. He told us a story to purposely make us afraid to walk back to our cars. I can't remember what it was though!

[Editor's Note: Stephen King had often used this tale to get his audience stirred up before an event… Look for "Sooner or Later" in this year's Calendar section.]

FEBRUARY

24 MONDAY

25 TUESDAY

26 WEDNESDAY

FILM REVIEW: I KNOW WHAT YOU NEED

Stephen King's short story, "I Know What You Need" was originally published in the September issue of Cosmopolitan magazine. It was later collected in King's 1978 *Night Shift*, his first short story collection. The story is about young college student, Elizabeth Rogan, who is cramming for a final exam when she meets fellow student, Ed Hamner, Jr. Ed is an outcast and a bit...different from the other students as he has a bit of paranormal ability to just "know things". He offers Elizabeth a strawberry ice cream as he knows this is on her mind, and she wants to take a break from studying. After he informs her he knows the answers to the final she's studying for; she later realizes he was helpful. Their relationship grows over several months and they become a couple, but something is wrong here...very wrong! Ed has a certain power over Elizabeth, one that would make her fall in love with him and become his.

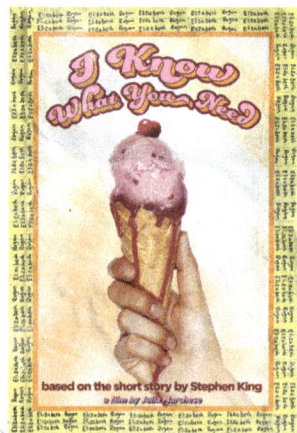

Poster Art by Mike Baird

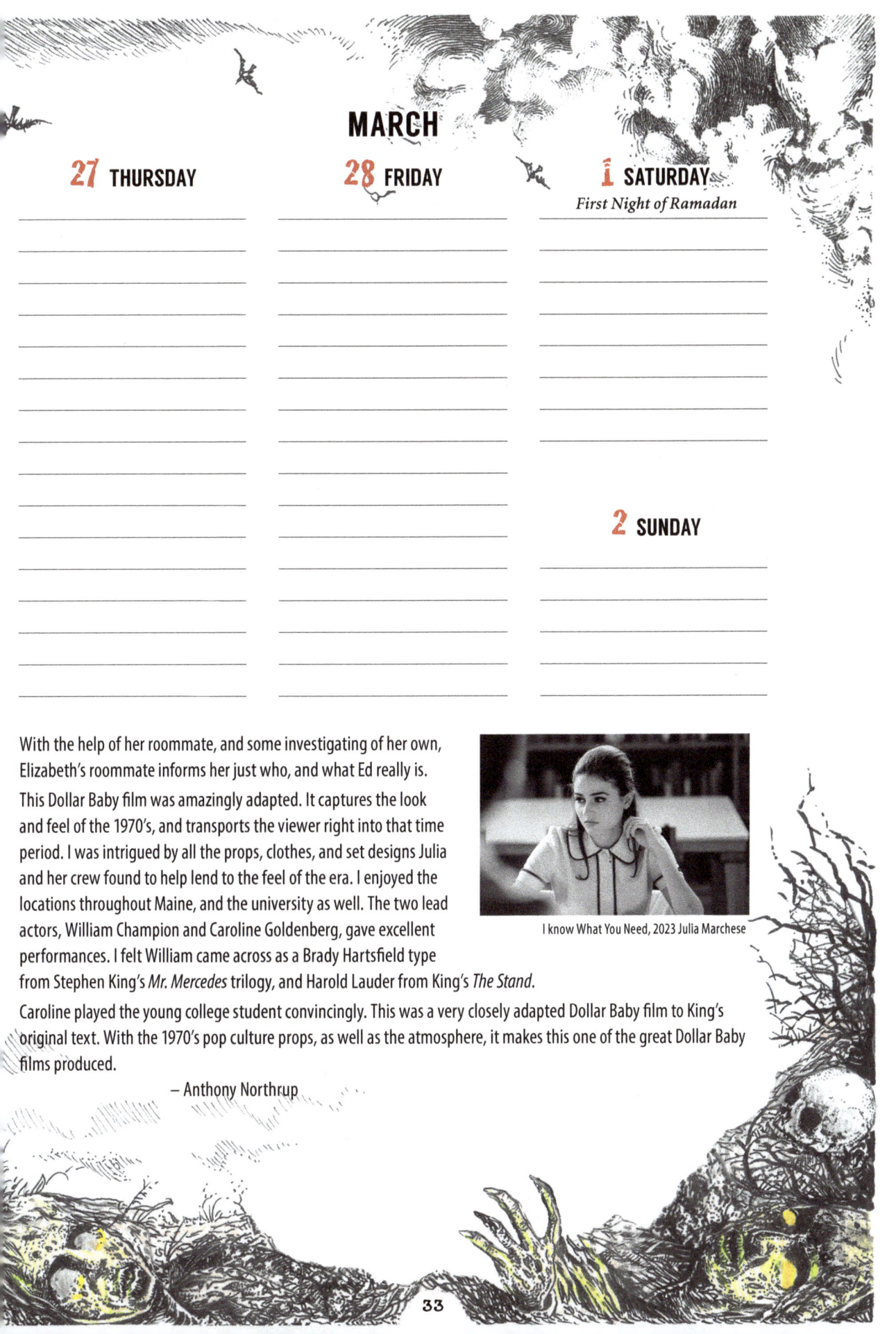

MARCH

27 THURSDAY

_____
_____
_____
_____
_____
_____
_____
_____
_____
_____
_____
_____
_____
_____
_____
_____
_____

28 FRIDAY

_____
_____
_____
_____
_____
_____
_____
_____
_____
_____
_____
_____
_____
_____
_____
_____
_____

1 SATURDAY
First Night of Ramadan

_____
_____
_____
_____
_____
_____
_____
_____
_____

2 SUNDAY

_____
_____
_____
_____
_____
_____
_____
_____

With the help of her roommate, and some investigating of her own, Elizabeth's roommate informs her just who, and what Ed really is.

This Dollar Baby film was amazingly adapted. It captures the look and feel of the 1970's, and transports the viewer right into that time period. I was intrigued by all the props, clothes, and set designs Julia and her crew found to help lend to the feel of the era. I enjoyed the locations throughout Maine, and the university as well. The two lead actors, William Champion and Caroline Goldenberg, gave excellent performances. I felt William came across as a Brady Hartsfield type from Stephen King's *Mr. Mercedes* trilogy, and Harold Lauder from King's *The Stand*.

I know What You Need, 2023 Julia Marchese

Caroline played the young college student convincingly. This was a very closely adapted Dollar Baby film to King's original text. With the 1970's pop culture props, as well as the atmosphere, it makes this one of the great Dollar Baby films produced.

— Anthony Northrup

MARCH

3 MONDAY

1958 Plymouth Fury stunt car used in *Christine*. This one in California (pictured), one in Florida and a promo *Christine* that was given away in a contest and now resides in England.

DO YOU REALLY. . . KNOW?

In the short story and Dollar Baby Film, I Know What You Need, one of the characters is a student by the name of Ed Hamner, Jr.

Who is this a reference to?

There is a Stephen King story / TV episode connection to Hamner, Jr. What are their two stories?

What did he create for in the mid-sixties?

He became well-known for a series based on his family and upbringing. What is this series?

MARCH

6 THURSDAY

_____
_____
_____
_____
_____
_____
_____
_____
_____
_____
_____
_____
_____

7 FRIDAY

_____
_____
_____
_____
_____
_____
_____
_____
_____
_____
_____
_____
_____

8 SATURDAY

_____
_____
_____
_____
_____

9 SUNDAY
Daylight Saving begins

_____
_____
_____
_____
_____

Answers:

A1: Earl Hamner, Jr., a writer in television. Featured in the original short story his full name in that is Edward Jackson Hamner, Jr. The fact that Stephen King added the "Jr." was a dead giveaway that this was a nod to Earl Hamner, Jr.

A2: Earl Hamner, Jr. wrote a *Twilight Zone* episode, "You Drive" (Season 5, Ep. 15), which features a man and his car that was involved in a hit and run. It seems his car has a mind of its own, a car with a conscience. This was used similarly two decades later in 1983 by Stephen King, in the evil *Christine*, albeit with its own unique way to solve its issues it has with others. Oliver Pope in this episode is haunted by his car and forced in the end to do right.

A3: Earl Hamner, Jr. wrote many *Twilight Zone* episodes, eight total. One of his most famous is "The Hunt," along with many supernatural themed episodes like "A Piano in the House" and "Jess-Belle."

A4: *The Waltons*. This show, along with the movie, *Spencer's Mountain* (starring Henry Fonda and Maureen O'Hara), was inspired by his childhood. Hamner introduced each show with a voice-over narration for most episodes. He also created *Falcon Crest*, another long running TV series. I'll be honest with you readers, I'm just happy to include Mr. Hamner here. He brought a lot of fun and enlightening entertainment to me and my family growing up. He left us in 2016 but he has quite a legacy of story telling in his wake. Look up his work sometime.

35

MARCH

10 MONDAY   **11** TUESDAY   **12** WEDNESDAY

Simpsons episode
"Please Homer,
Don't Hammer 'Em"
S. 18 Ep 3,
featuring The Rock
Bottom Remainders.

ROCK N' WRITE, ALL NIGHT LONG

The Rock Bottom Remainder's personnel list
From 1993 this is the original lineup of the authors, artists, and co-conspirators that began this unique musical trek.

DAVE BARRY, lead guitar, vocals

TAD BARTIMUS, Remainderette

LORRAINE BATTLE, wardrobe, shop till you drop

ROY BLOUNT, JR., Critics Chorus and master of ceremonies

BOB DAITZ, tour manager, scapegoat, non-navigator, Sammy you should see me now

BOB DANNIC, universal crew, driver

MICHAEL DORRIS, percussion (Anaheim and Bottom Line only)

CAROLE EITINGON, concessions, merchandising, life of the party

JIM ENGLAND, guitar technician, mysterious man from Maine

ROBERT FULGHUM, mandocello, vocals

KATHI KAMEN GOLDMARK, Remainderette and Founding Mom

MATT GROENING, Critics Chorus

HOOVER (CHRIS RANKIN), production manager, sound engineer, good shorts

JOSH KELLY, drums, best attitude in the biz (and the bus)

STEPHEN KING, rhythm guitar, vocals

MARCH

13 THURSDAY

14 FRIDAY

15 SATURDAY

16 SUNDAY

TABITHA KING, tour photographer, shop till you drop

BARBARA KINGSOLVER, keyboards, vocals

AL KOOPER, musical director, guitar, keyboards, vocals, video expert

GREIL MARCUS, Critics Chorus

DAVE MARSH, Critics Chorus, Teen Angel

MOUSE (DANNY DELALUZ), keyboard/drum technician, lead flashlight

RIDLEY PEARSON, bass guitar, vocals, Designated Worrier

JERRY PETERSON, saxophone, "Check it out!"

JOEL SELVIN, Critics Chorus, lead scream

AMY TAN, Remainderette, Rhythm Dominatrix

JIMMY VIVINO, keyboards, vocals

DAVE WORTERS, bus driver, tour guide

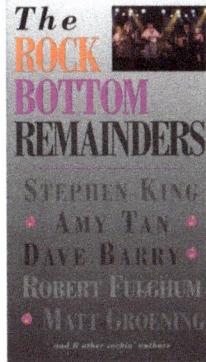

The Rock Bottom
Remainders
VHS 1993
BMG Video

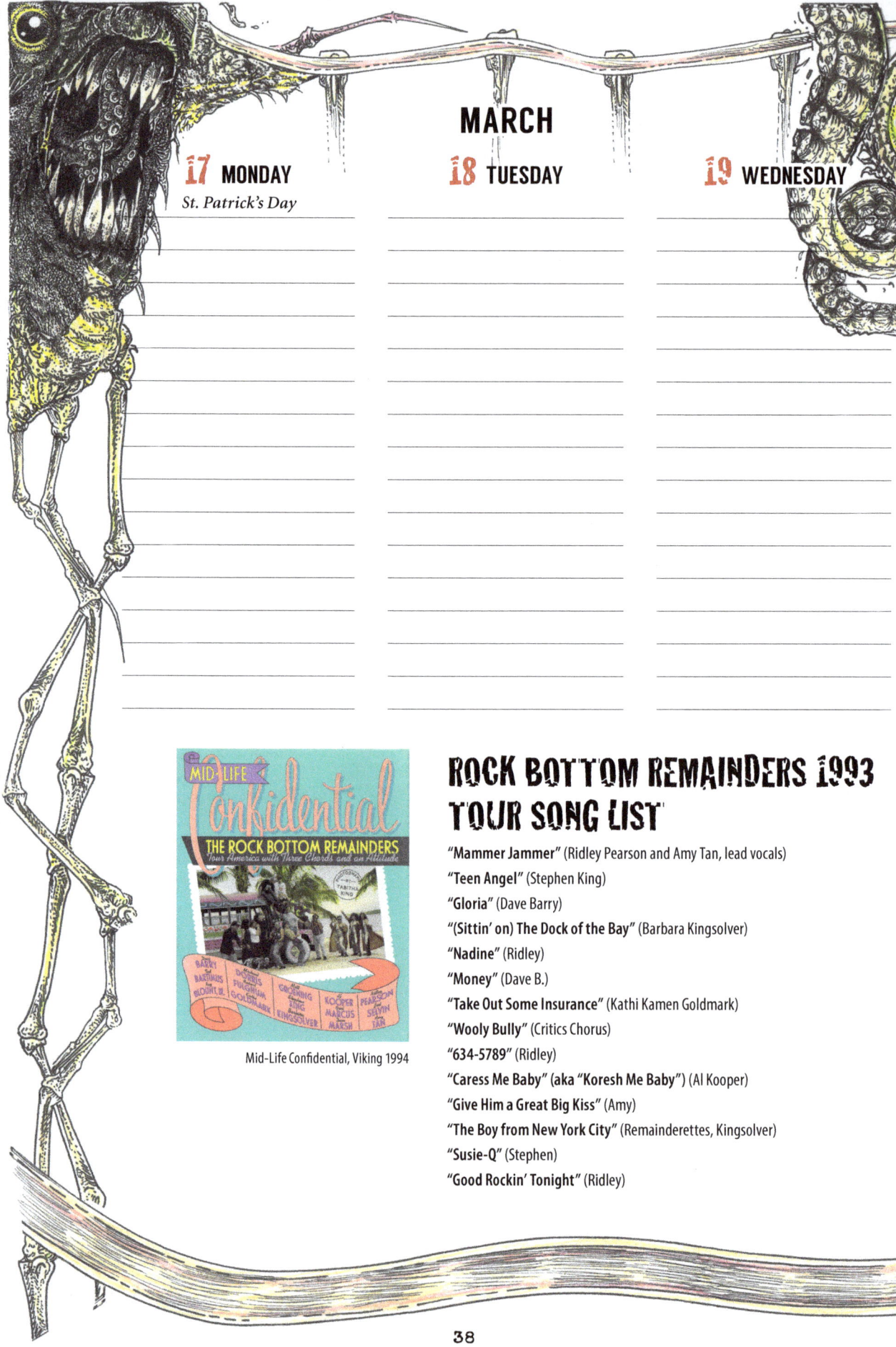

17 MONDAY
St. Patrick's Day

18 TUESDAY

19 WEDNESDAY

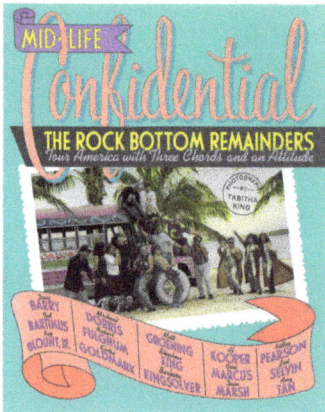

Mid-Life Confidential, Viking 1994

ROCK BOTTOM REMAINDERS 1993 TOUR SONG LIST

"Mammer Jammer" (Ridley Pearson and Amy Tan, lead vocals)

"Teen Angel" (Stephen King)

"Gloria" (Dave Barry)

"(Sittin' on) The Dock of the Bay" (Barbara Kingsolver)

"Nadine" (Ridley)

"Money" (Dave B.)

"Take Out Some Insurance" (Kathi Kamen Goldmark)

"Wooly Bully" (Critics Chorus)

"634-5789" (Ridley)

"Caress Me Baby" (aka **"Koresh Me Baby"**) (Al Kooper)

"Give Him a Great Big Kiss" (Amy)

"The Boy from New York City" (Remainderettes, Kingsolver)

"Susie-Q" (Stephen)

"Good Rockin' Tonight" (Ridley)

MARCH

20 THURSDAY

21 FRIDAY

22 SATURDAY

23 SUNDAY

"Stand by Me" (Stephen)

"Louie Louie" (Critics Chorus; Joel Selvin, scream solo)

"You Can't Sit Down" (Kathi)

"The Last Time" (Dave B.)

"Who Do You Love" (Stephen)

"Land of 1,000 Dances" (Dave B.)

"Last Kiss" (Stephen)

"Leader of the Pack" (Amy)

"Double Shot (Of My Baby's Love)" (Critics Chorus)

"He Will Break Your Heart" (Dave B., Kathi)

"My Guy" (Tad Bartimus)

"Chain of Fools" (Tad)

"These Boots Are Made for Walkin'" (Amy)

"Endless Sleep" (Stephen)

"Midnight Hour" (Ridley)

"Short Shorts" (Critics Chorus; Remainderettes)

Source: *Mid-Life Confidential* 1994 Viking hardcover.

Stand By Me Soundtrack, Japanese, 2012

MARCH

I SAW SUE KISSING STEPHEN KING

The story of these photos actually starts 13 years earlier. On 9/22/1998 the novel *Bag Of Bones* dropped. On 9/29/1998 thousands of fans gathered at the the Harold Washington Library in downtown Chicago for Stephen King's stop on a tightly scheduled tour. The decision was made to put him at a table on the ground floor, to sit at the table "take book - look up and smile - sign Book - hand book to a gentleman that would hand the book back to the fan." Then gently guide said fan out of the way. This routine was so mechanical, so sterile. And I felt so bad for Mr. King.

Photo: Sue Marcus

When my turn came, I needed to shake things up a little. Before he could look up at me, I positioned a small gift I had brought for him (pertaining to Chicago) right on the unsigned book. He looked at the gift, then looked me as I explained what it was while we discussed it for a moment. Then, something I said, made his body guards jump! The four of us had a fun moment in conversation. This whole interaction with the men took much longer than the others before me... some staff in charge of "The Machine" were a little bent out of shape because of this.

He signed my book then as I walked away, I felt fantastic with our interactions. I had slowed him down just a bit and produced a small breather for him. But then a nagging thought crept in... it would have been perfection if I had only touched him. Doing that small gesture, would have been a little bit more personal (and memorable for me).

MARCH

21 THURSDAY

----

28 FRIDAY

----

29 SATURDAY

----

30 SUNDAY

11/31/2011. The Rock Bottom Remainder's had a Chicago concert on their schedule. There was also an option to attend a Meet & Greet Event at another location before their show. I brought only one book with me for possible signatures & photos: *Mid-Life Confidential* (FYI the book was written by the original band members, formed by Kathy Goldmark. With each member writing a chapter about their own experiences). The Remainders arrive, and as you can imagine, Stepen King was singled out and swarmed by the fans! He was very thin and pale from the van accident in 1999 (where King has stated he keeps weight off to keep the pressure off his leg, thus his look). A huge line was formed in front of him, with people waiting to get their books signed, and I mean, books bought before the event. It didn't matter that they were later printings, in hardcover or even paperback. People with books piled high in their arms. Really disturbing to me. There was another room where the rest of the band members hung out so that's where I went. I was busy greeting all of them. These authors are all great as far as I'm concerned. After I was done I sat at a table and visited with Amy Tan, her husband Lou, & Tabitha King.

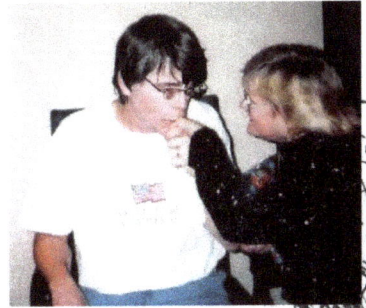

Photo: Sue Marcus

She hogged my book re-reading her chapter. When finished she looked up and said, "Huh, no wonder my books aren't selling". I would excuse myself to go check on the King line in the next room here and there. FINALLY, the line was small enough to join it.

I asked a friend, as I handed him my camera, "Take as many photos as if your life depended on it." And he did just that. MY TURN! Finally, to sit with The Master. So, as we talked, he signed his chapter in my Remainder book. Our subject being about his Chicago book signing in 1998. And almost, as an after-thought, I pointed my finger at him, and said: "You know what? All those years ago in Chicago, as I walked away from the signing line, I had such a sad thought. I Just WANTED to TOUCH your hand." With that being said, he held and lifted my pointed finger hand… AND KISSED it!

My heart just melted. I will never be able to forget this evening, or that sweet kiss.

— Sue Marcus

APRIL

31 MONDAY

1 TUESDAY
April Fools' Day

2 WEDNESDAY

SOONER OR LATER. . .

"I was going through some insurance actuarial figures, for car insurance, and discovered that one in every 50 people, when they come to an event like this, forget to lock their car and anybody could get into the back. I don't say that that's going to happen here or anything, but somebody could and that's almost like a public service. So, if you see a face in your mirror on the way home. . . and here's the thing, everybody's laughing about it now, when they're all together, but sooner or later, you'll be by yourself, in your car. . ."

– Stephen King, John F. Kennedy Sixth Floor Museum event, Majestic Theatre, Dallas, Texas
November 10, 2011

Stephen King told this story many times at speaking events over the years to keep the audience thinking. . . all the way to their cars, and beyond!

The gift that keeps on giving. . .

LEE COLLUM
Journalist, KERA

STEPHEN KING
Novelist

jfk.org

2011 Conversation with Stephen King, JFK.org

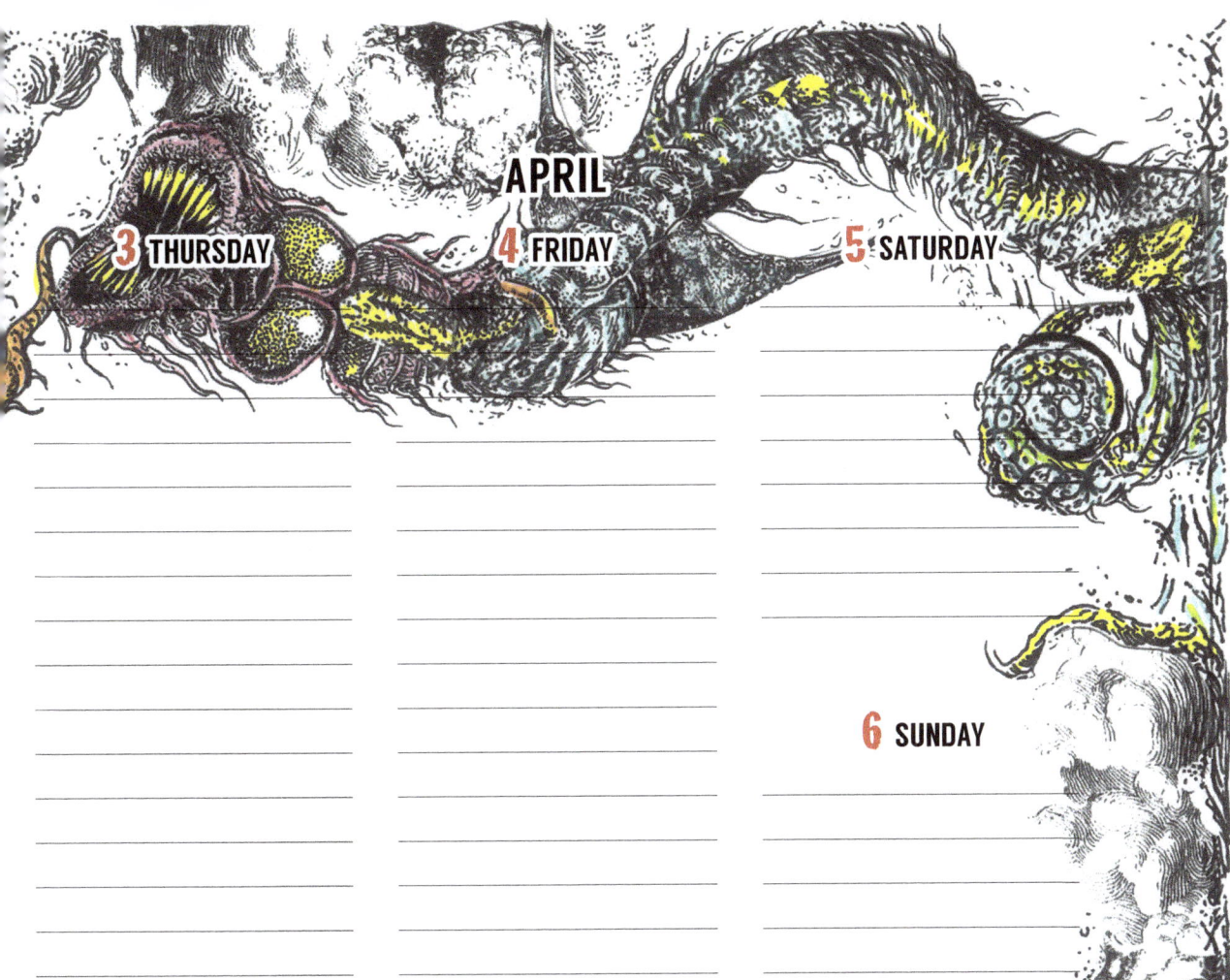

APRIL

3 THURSDAY

4 FRIDAY

5 SATURDAY

6 SUNDAY

On November 22, 1963, President John F. Kennedy was assassinated in downtown Dallas.

If you had the chance to change history, would you?

Stephen King's novel *11/22/63* addresses this very scenario as the book's main character travels back in time on a mission to prevent the assassination of President Kennedy.

Stephen King's novel, *11-22-63*, was released on November 8th, 2011. It only seemed fitting that Stephen King was front and center at a fundraiser at the Majestic Theatre in Dallas on Thursday, November 10, 2011, benefiting The Sixth Floor Museum at Dealey Plaza. There was an exclusive reception that featured the author at 5:45 p.m. A conversation was facilitated by Dallas columnist and broadcaster Lee Cullum at 7 PM for an hour-long discussion in front of a sold-out audience.

2012 Scribner press, US

7 MONDAY

8 TUESDAY

9 WEDNESDAY

THREE KINGS

April 4, 2008 — Nearly five hundred fans and Constant Readers gathered at the Lutheran Church of the Reformation for the PEN/Faulkner Foundation presentation of The Three Kings: Stephen, Tabitha, and Owen King. The event was part of the PEN/Faulkner Literary Reading Series in association with the Folger Shakespeare Library.

My wife had bought tickets for us as a birthday present for me. It was the first time I met Stephen King, my literary idol since I was 13 years old and saw the 'Salem's Lot miniseries. Afterwards I immediately read the book, and

Fri. Apr 04, 2008   8:00 PM   00128638
PEN/FAULKNER FOUNDATION
STEPHEN KING, TABITHA KING AND OWEN KING
Folger Theatre
201 East Capitol Street SE   INETFULL
Washington, DC 20003 $30.00
                                    +$3.50 INETFEE
Folger Box Office (202) 544-7077
GENERAL ADMISSION   400609

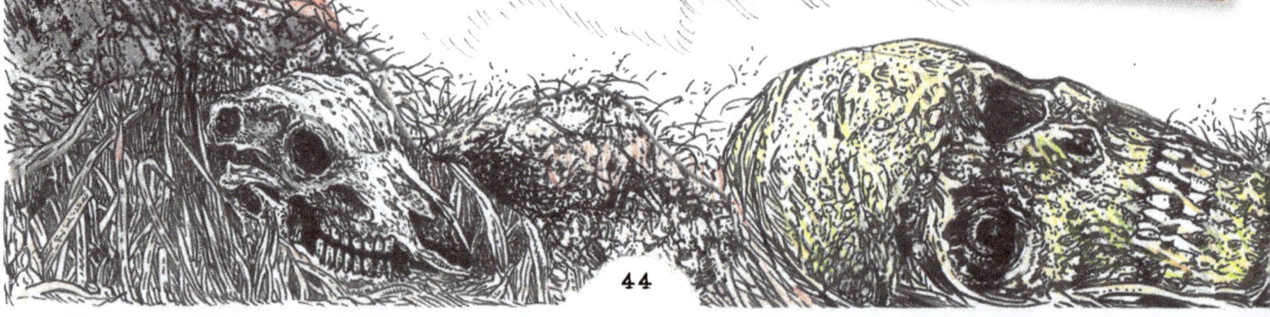

APRIL

10 THURSDAY

_____
_____
_____
_____
_____
_____
_____
_____
_____
_____
_____
_____
_____

11 FRIDAY

_____
_____
_____
_____
_____
_____
_____
_____
_____
_____
_____
_____
_____

12 SATURDAY
Passover

_____
_____
_____
_____
_____
_____

13 SUNDAY
Palm Sunday

_____
_____
_____
_____
_____
_____

eventually read the rest of Stephen King's published work. And on top of that, it was an opportunity to meet his wife and youngest son, marvelous authors in their own rights.

The reading portion of the event took place in the Lutheran church as the Folger Library did not have room for the crowd. The night opened with Tabitha King reading from a novel in progress. Owen followed, reading his short story "Nothing is in Bad Taste," a beautifully written tale of a souring relationship. I've wanted to read the story several times since then, but it has yet to be collected. Finally, Stephen read the opening chapter of his yet-to-be-published novel, _Under the Dome_. The fate of that woodchuck haunted everybody.

Following the reading, the crowd moved across the street to the Folger Shakespeare Library, where each writer agreed to sign one book for each fan. I brought along _Creepshow_ and _Cycle of the Werewolf_. Not having anything in my library by Tabby or Owen, I had them sign the program.

An exciting, wonderful, and very memorable night.

— T. L. Emery

PEN/FAULKNER

PEN/Faulkner presents

The Three Kings
Stephen, Tabitha and Owen King

Introduction by Mary Kay Zuravleff

Friday, April 4, 2008
8:00 PM
Folger Shakespeare Library
Washington, D.C.

NATIONAL
ENDOWMENT
FOR THE ARTS

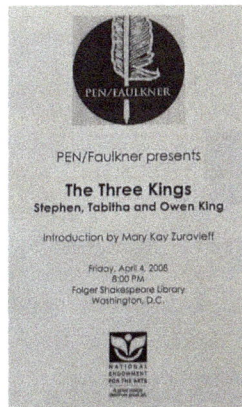

The Three Kings Program Booklet
PEN/Faulkner event
April 4th, 2008

14 MONDAY

15 TUESDAY
Tax Day

16 WEDNESDAY

HOPE SPRINGS ETERNAL

I have been a Stephen King fan from the beginning. I read *Carrie* and was hooked and always tried to get the next book as soon as available. I moved to the Canadian Forces Base (CFB) in Lahr/Schwartzwald, Germany in 1975 and wondered how I would get my Stephen King books. Fortunately, there was an American Book Store on the Base and I would run in and order new books as soon as I learned about them. With the Book Store and a Doubleday Book Club membership (not my favorite but at least it was books), I survived the four years in Germany!

I returned to Canada in 1979 and we were posted to CFB Gagetown, Oromocto, New Brunswick. I was so excited when I observed how close we were to Bangor, Maine! I worked at the Base and each Canadian Thanksgiving about 14 of my female colleagues and I would plan a trip to Bangor for a "Girls Trip" and some early Christmas shopping. I always hoped to run into Stephen King but it never happened, that is... until 1982. Our daughters were allowed to come when they were 14 years old and so my daughter, Lezlie, was on this trip. We left on Friday, October 8th and went straight to the Bangor Mall to do some early shopping. I was so excited when I saw the sign at B. Dalton Bookseller that Stephen King

B. Dalton, Bangor, Maine, 1982

APRIL

17 THURSDAY

_____
_____
_____
_____
_____
_____
_____
_____
_____
_____
_____
_____
_____
_____

18 FRIDAY
Good Friday

_____
_____
_____
_____
_____
_____
_____
_____
_____
_____
_____
_____
_____

19 SATURDAY

_____
_____
_____
_____
_____
_____

20 SUNDAY
Easter

_____
_____
_____
_____
_____
_____

would be there, in person, on Saturday and I knew where I would be. That evening we met my colleagues for a late dinner and that was all I could talk about–they were less enthused as they were not avid fans!

On that Saturday we were at the Bangor Mall early and I was about the fifth person in line for the book signing. Stephen was so charming to everyone ahead of me and then finally it was my turn. Stephen asked my name and signed my copy of *Different Seasons*. I then asked Stephen if I could take his photo and he said of course he didn't mind. My daughter was waiting with the camera and took his photo. Stephen then asked if the photo was for me and when I said yes he said "well get in the photo too" – I was thrilled and that is how I have the treasured photo of Stephen King and me.

Photo: Fran MacBride

When I say treasured, I truly mean that. I kept the photos in my jewellery box for many years, I knew that in the event of a fire the first thing I would grab was my jewellery box! Eventually, as technology improved, I scanned the photos in 2014 as they bring back such great memories.

In closing, prior to COVID I wintered in Fort Myers, Florida. I remain a constant fan and I knew that Stephen and Tabitha King had a home in Sarasota and hoped to possibly see him on my visits there, but it was not to be. And, my daughter warned me that lurking around could be considered stalking!

Who knows perhaps I will see him again one day, some 40+ years after my first experience.

– Fran MacBride, 2024, Canada

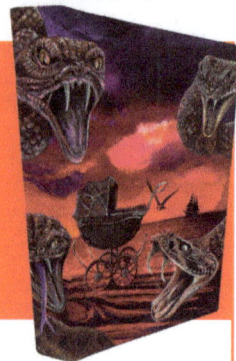

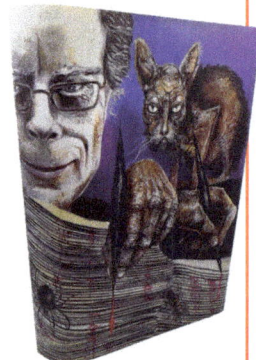

49

APRIL

21 MONDAY

22 TUESDAY
Earth Day

23 WEDNESDAY

DO YOU REMEMBER ROCK N' ROLL RADIO?

Musician and producer Al Kooper joined up with The Rock Bottom Remainders, not only to help on keyboards and play guitar, but he was their musician mentor and helped shore up the authors-turned-musicians to become a band.

Al Kooper is a very famous musician. He has written, performed, and produced many bands, albums, and toured with artists. Can you name 3 or more artists that he has any association with?

Al Kooper played French horn, organ, and piano on what famous song by the Rolling Stones?

Al Kooper discovered, signed, and then produced albums, by what famous southern band?

How did Al Kooper end up joining The Rock Bottom Remainders in their early days?

mid-life **CONFIDENTIAL**

STARRING

Dave Barry, Tad Bartimus, Roy Blount, Jr., Michael Dorris, Robert Fulghum, Kathi Goldmark, Matt Groening, Stephen King, Tabitha King, Barbara Kingsolver, Al Kooper, Greil Marcus, Dave Marsh, Ridley Pearson, Joel Selvin, Amy Tan

Hodder & Stoughton
1994, UK Edition

APRIL

24 THURSDAY

25 FRIDAY

26 SATURDAY

27 SUNDAY

Answers:

A1: Kooper has played on hundreds of records, including ones by the Rolling Stones, B.B. King, the Who, the Jimi Hendrix Experience, Alice Cooper, Stephen Stills, Mike Bloomfield, and Cream. He lived next to Jimi Hendrix and they played together often. He also created the band Blood, Sweat, and Tears, but left after the first album.

A2: "You Can't Always Get What You Want." It was named as the 100th greatest song of all time by *Rolling Stone* magazine in its 2004 list of the "500 Greatest Songs of All Time."

A3: Lynyrd Skynyrd. Kooper produced their first three albums.

A4: After his release of *Backstage Passes* (his autobiography) this qualified him as a member of the Rock Bottom Remainders. Look up Al Kooper, this is a small fraction of how he's impacted the music universe.

Al Kooper and Stephen King Performing with the Rock Bottom Remainders

28 MONDAY

29 TUESDAY

30 WEDNESDAY

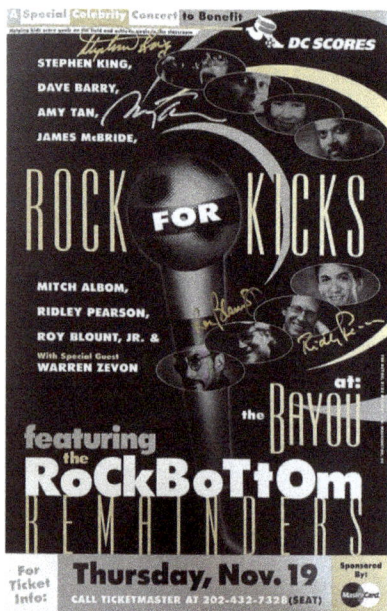

1998 The Bayou Theater, Bayou, Washington, D.C.

DOWN ON THE BAYOU

ROCK BOTTOM REMAINDERS
SIGNED 1998 POSTER - AT THE BAYOU, D.C.

An original concert poster for the "Rock Bottom Remainders" performing on November 19, 1998 at The Bayou in Washington, D.C. as a benefit for a charity called "DC Scores". The "Rock Bottom Remainders" was a rock band made up of a revolving group of famous authors that would convene to perform charity concerts. The five authors/performers who are listed and pictured on, and SIGNED, this particular poster are: STEPHEN KING, DAVE BARRY, AMY TAN, ROY BLOUNT, JR. and RIDLEY PEARSON. Also pictured and listed on this poster but who did not sign were Mitch Albom and "Special Guest" Warren Zevon! The size of this poster is approximately 11" x 17.125" on medium-thick glossy paper.

MAY

1 THURSDAY

2 FRIDAY

3 SATURDAY
Kentucky Derby Day

4 SUNDAY
Cinco de Mayo

Can you guess which authors have autographed this copy of *Mid-Life Confidential*?

Answers:

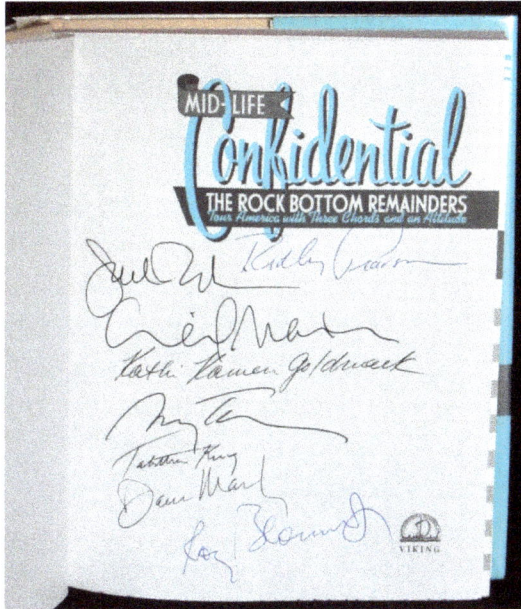

Mid-Life Confidential, Viking 1994

Line 1: Joel Selvin; Ridley Pearson
Line 2: Greil Marcus
Line 3: Kathi Kamen Goldmark
Line 4: Amy Tan
Line 5: Tabitha King
Line 6: Dave Marsh
Line 7: Roy Blount, Jr.

MAY

5 MONDAY
Cinco de Mayo

6 TUESDAY

7 WEDNESDAY

SOLD MORE BOOKS THAN THE BEATLES!

ROCK BOTTOM REMAINDERS REVIEW – April 21, 2010, 9:30 Club.

Music reviewer for the Washington, D.C. area, Michael Darpino, published his account of seeing The Rock Bottom Remainders at the 9:30 Club and declared it "one of the weirdest concerts I have ever attended." He also said it was "one of the most unique and unlikely cover bands of all time." His obvious interest in the music scene, being a music reporter for the area, brought him to this very unlikely event with this group of heavy hitter authors there up on stage. Featuring Scott Turow, Amy Tan, Dave Barry, and Mitch Albom. He also noted that the Remainders MC, Roy Blount Jr. mentioned that "they are the only band that has sold more books that The Beatles."

Who's going to debate that?

Mr. Darpino, who'd previously worked in a local bookstore, never imagined he'd actually see this band, much less locally. This was the

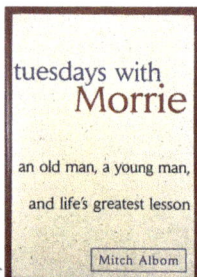

Tuesdays with Morrie
Doubleday 1997

54

MAY

8 THURSDAY

_____
_____
_____
_____
_____
_____
_____
_____
_____
_____
_____
_____
_____
_____
_____

9 FRIDAY

_____
_____
_____
_____
_____
_____
_____
_____
_____
_____
_____
_____
_____
_____
_____

10 SATURDAY

_____
_____
_____
_____
_____
_____
_____

11 SUNDAY

Mother's Day

_____
_____
_____
_____
_____

2010 Wordstock Tour that had The Rock Bottom Remainders conducting a short East Coast tour to benefit World Vision's efforts on behalf of Haiti relief. The band also shared proceeds with local causes in the cities they performed in. In DC they gave to the Washington-based America's Promise Alliance; and We Give Books, donating 5 books per ticket-sold to DC Public Schools.

He also mentioned that "this band had a kind of mythical status as stories of their rare sightings were told by my co-workers as if they were akin to the Loch Ness Monster or Big Foot." Yes, I think we could all relate seeing these author's milling about in any of our locales would have been quite a pleasant surprise!

He also recounted that MC, Blount, told an anecdote of an old performance when during a Frank McCourt performance he was "singing one Beatles song while the band was playing another!" This is what happens at a concert where "some of

The Joy Luck Club 1989
G.P. Putnam's Sons

55

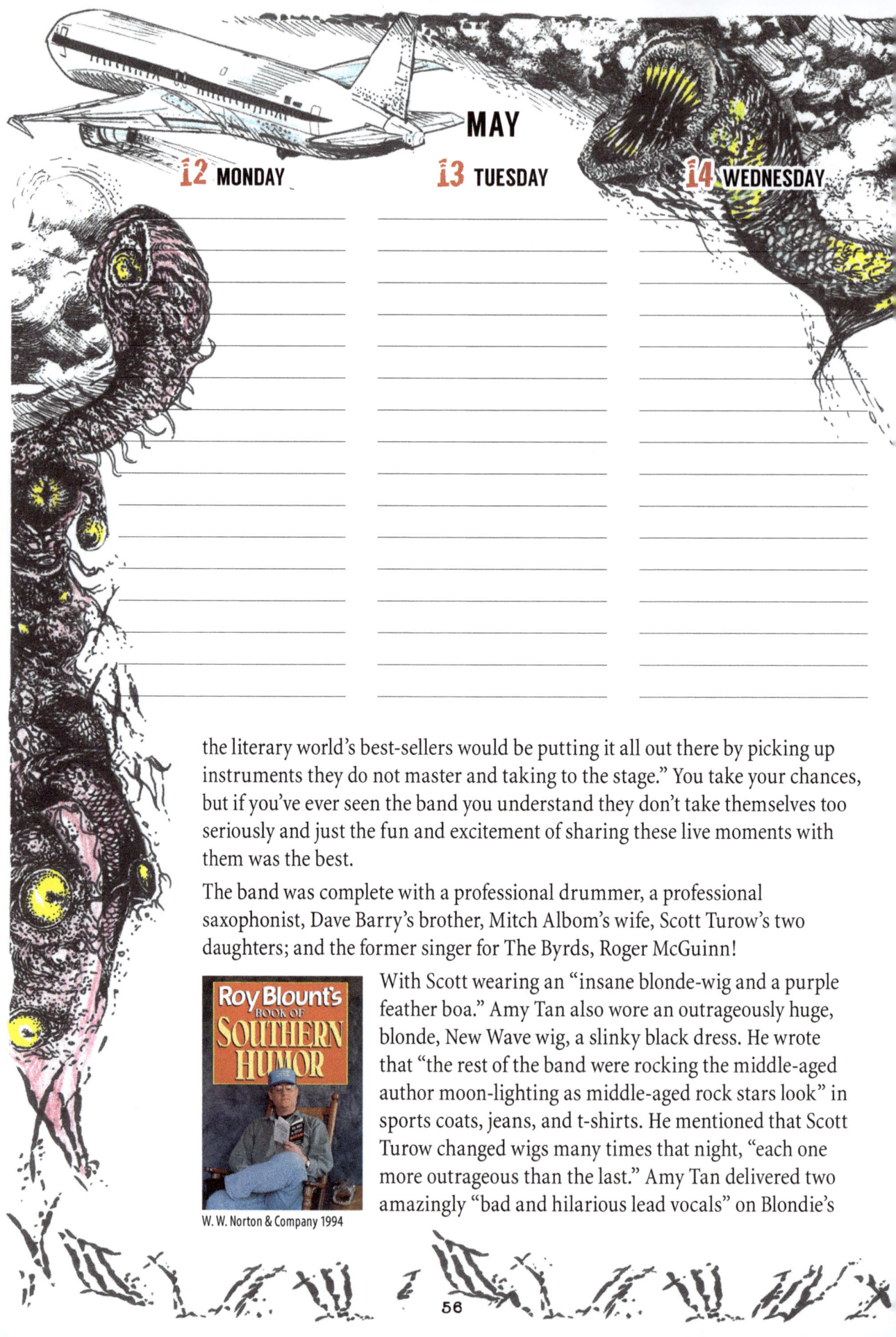

MAY

12 MONDAY

13 TUESDAY

14 WEDNESDAY

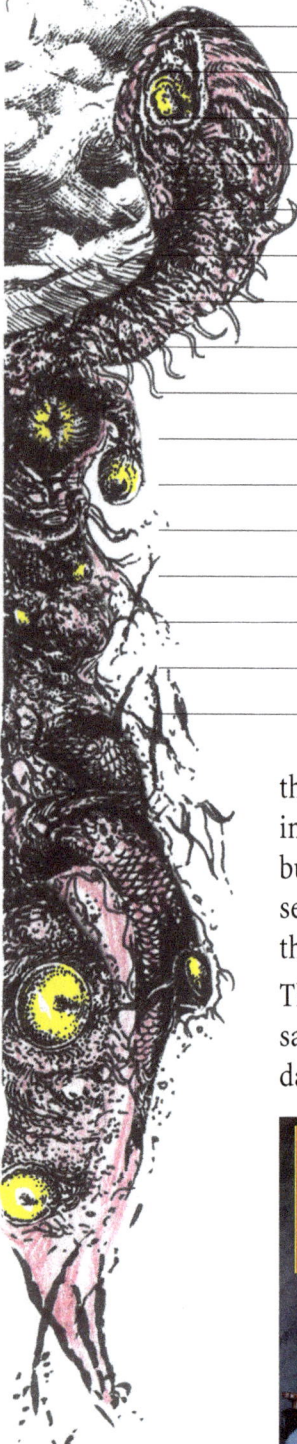

the literary world's best-sellers would be putting it all out there by picking up instruments they do not master and taking to the stage." You take your chances, but if you've ever seen the band you understand they don't take themselves too seriously and just the fun and excitement of sharing these live moments with them was the best.

The band was complete with a professional drummer, a professional saxophonist, Dave Barry's brother, Mitch Albom's wife, Scott Turow's two daughters; and the former singer for The Byrds, Roger McGuinn!

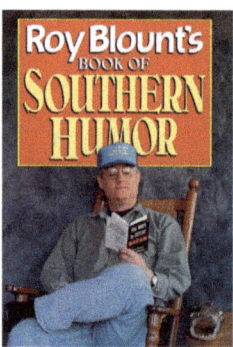

Roy Blount's BOOK OF SOUTHERN HUMOR

W. W. Norton & Company 1994

With Scott wearing an "insane blonde-wig and a purple feather boa." Amy Tan also wore an outrageously huge, blonde, New Wave wig, a slinky black dress. He wrote that "the rest of the band were rocking the middle-aged author moon-lighting as middle-aged rock stars look" in sports coats, jeans, and t-shirts. He mentioned that Scott Turow changed wigs many times that night, "each one more outrageous than the last." Amy Tan delivered two amazingly "bad and hilarious lead vocals" on Blondie's

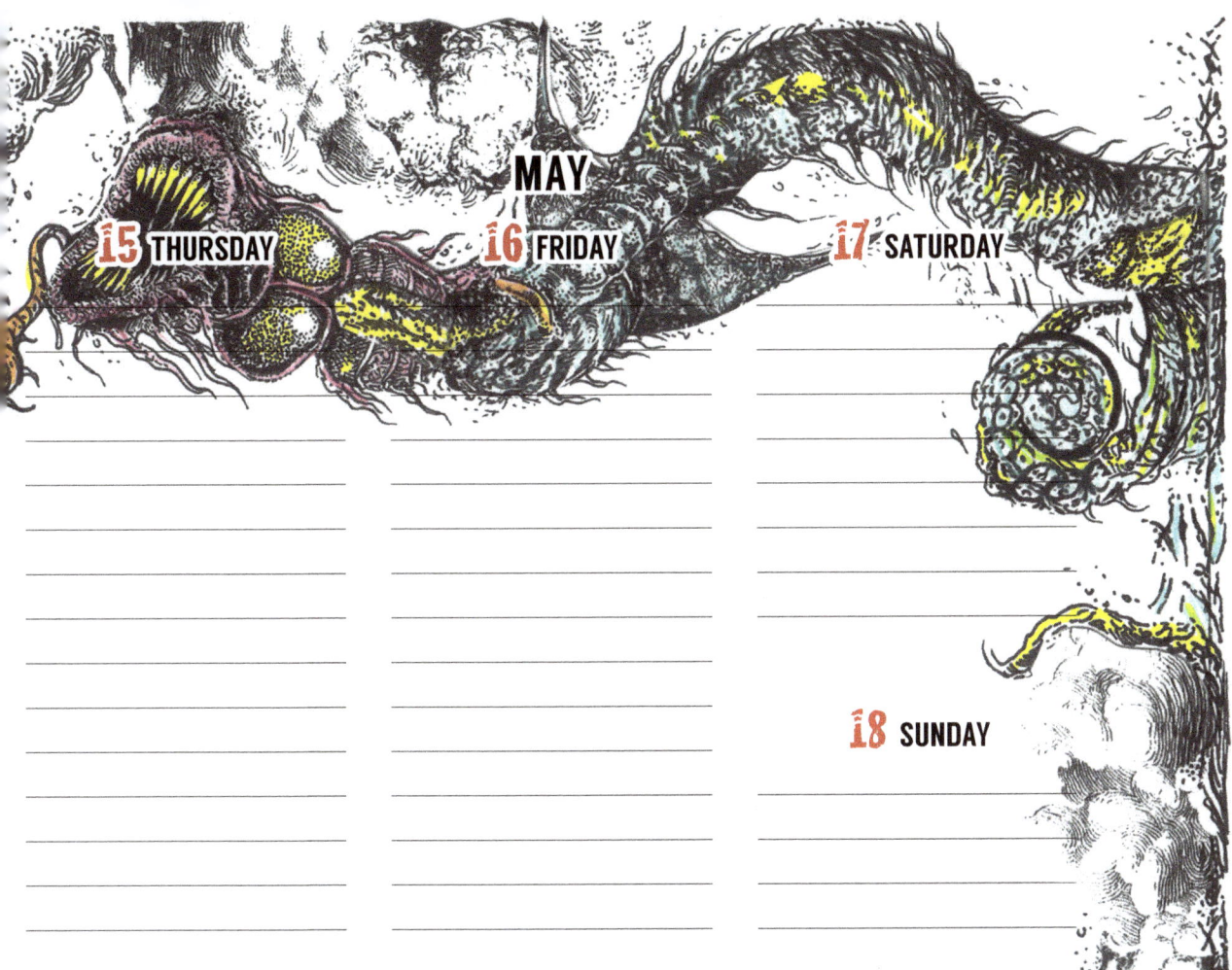

15 THURSDAY   **16** FRIDAY   **17** SATURDAY

18 SUNDAY

'One Way Or Another', wearing slit-glasses, and The Shangri-La's 'Leader of the Pack', her husband as the motorcycle rebel. Mitch Albom delivered an incredible two-song Elvis tribute with a gold-jacket era Elvis, complete with an Elvis wig and sunglasses. During 'Jail House Rock', Albom then "turned his back to the crowd and hip swiveled right down to his t-shirt and boxer shorts!"

Roger McGuinn was the band's special guest and Roy Blount Jr. noted, that McGuinn was invited to "remind the audience what good music sounds like". He played The Bryds' hits 'Mr. Tambourine Man' and 'Turn! Turn! Turn!', along with three more.

It's obvious the night was special and a really good time for some very good causes. Michael Darpino wrote "these literary titans turned tongue-in-cheek rock-gods in concert was something I never expected to have the opportunity to experience... it was a funny, surreal evening and I am very glad that I was there." A unique show for anyone who's experienced it as I have in Atlanta, back in 1993.

– Dave Hinchberger

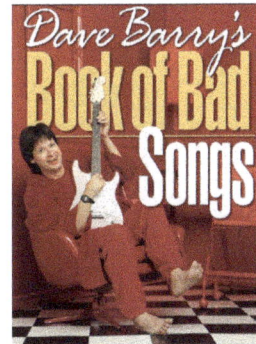

Andrews McMeel Publishing 2000

57

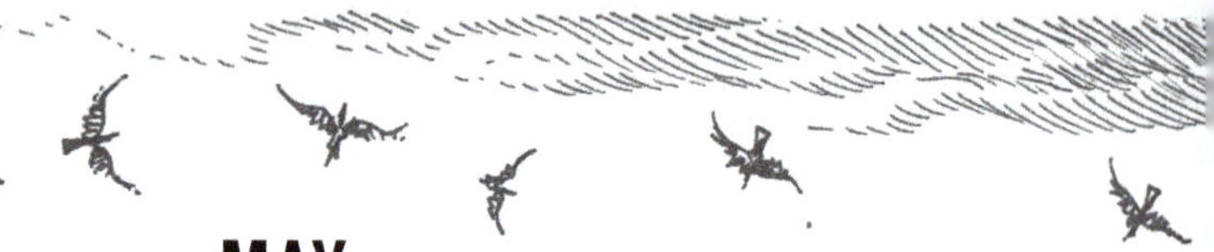

MAY

BOOK REVIEW

The Ideal, Genuine Man, by Don Robertson

When I think of Don Robertson, Stephen King invariably comes to mind. King always cited Robertson, along with John D. McDonald and Richard Matheson, as his biggest influences. I would never have read Don Robertson if it weren't for King.

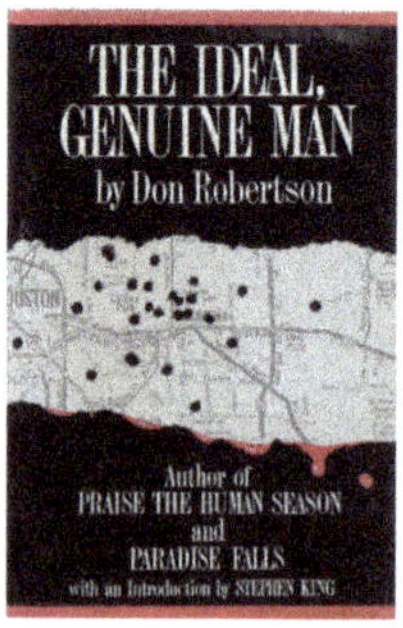

People are quick to draw comparisons of Thornton Wilder to *'Salem's Lot,* but I see more Don Robertson in the novel. Castle Rock wouldn't be the place we all know and fear without Robertson's *Paradise Falls.* The humanity in King's writing, the earthiness, the humor, the intricacies of human life. It's all there in the work of Don Robertson.

My first Don Robertson was *The Ideal, Genuine Man.* I read a battered paperback when I was, I think, thirty-one years old. I was amazed by the novel. Now I've

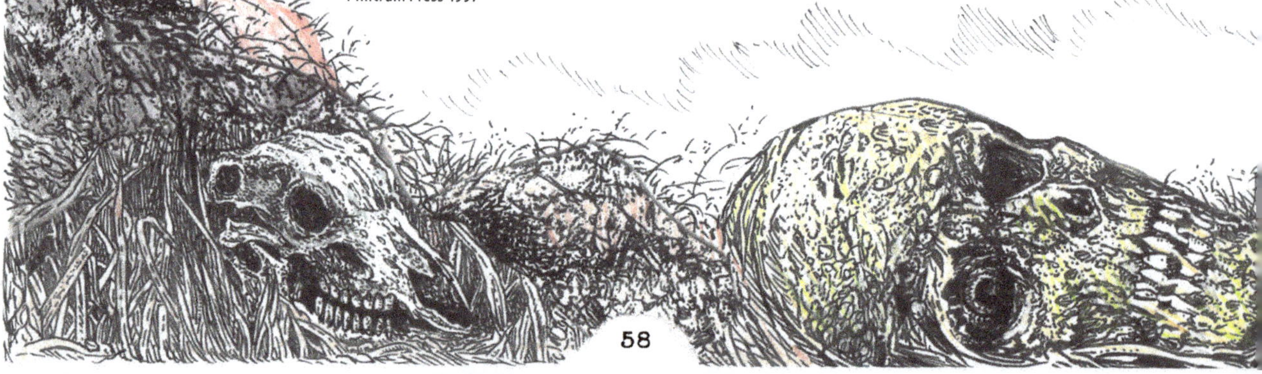

THE IDEAL, GENUINE MAN
by Don Robertson

Author of
PRAISE THE HUMAN SEASON
and
PARADISE FALLS
with an Introduction by STEPHEN KING

Philtrum Press 1997

58

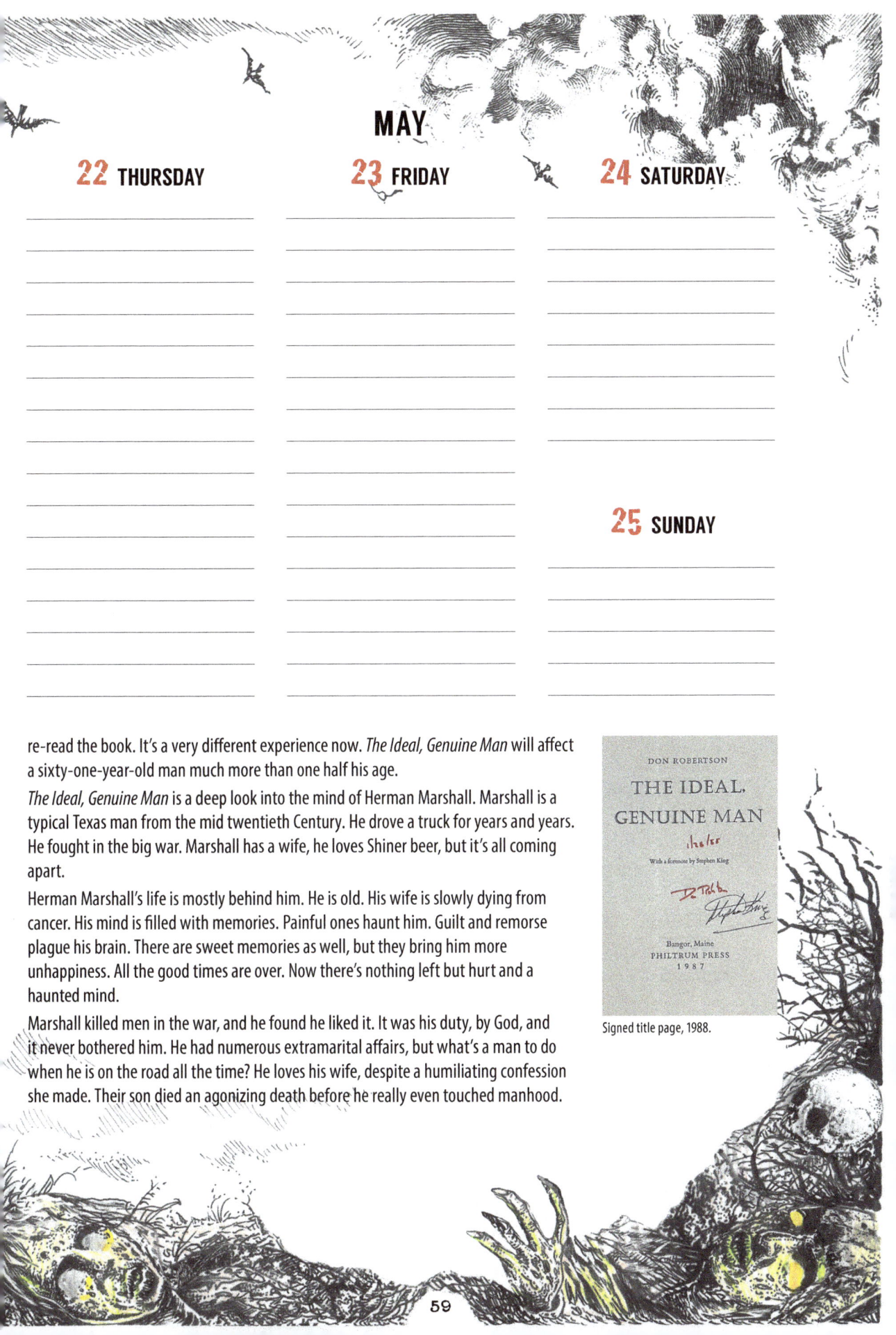

MAY

22 THURSDAY

_____
_____
_____
_____
_____
_____
_____
_____
_____
_____
_____
_____
_____
_____
_____
_____

23 FRIDAY

_____
_____
_____
_____
_____
_____
_____
_____
_____
_____
_____
_____
_____
_____
_____
_____

24 SATURDAY

_____
_____
_____
_____
_____
_____
_____

25 SUNDAY

_____
_____
_____
_____
_____
_____
_____

re-read the book. It's a very different experience now. _The Ideal, Genuine Man_ will affect a sixty-one-year-old man much more than one half his age.

The Ideal, Genuine Man is a deep look into the mind of Herman Marshall. Marshall is a typical Texas man from the mid twentieth Century. He drove a truck for years and years. He fought in the big war. Marshall has a wife, he loves Shiner beer, but it's all coming apart.

Herman Marshall's life is mostly behind him. He is old. His wife is slowly dying from cancer. His mind is filled with memories. Painful ones haunt him. Guilt and remorse plague his brain. There are sweet memories as well, but they bring him more unhappiness. All the good times are over. Now there's nothing left but hurt and a haunted mind.

Marshall killed men in the war, and he found he liked it. It was his duty, by God, and it never bothered him. He had numerous extramarital affairs, but what's a man to do when he is on the road all the time? He loves his wife, despite a humiliating confession she made. Their son died an agonizing death before he really even touched manhood.

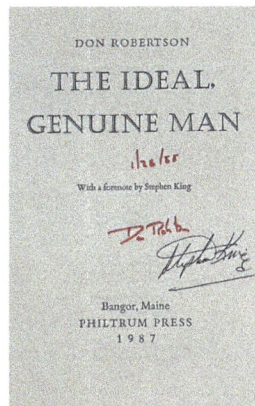

DON ROBERTSON

THE IDEAL,
GENUINE MAN

With a foreword by Stephen King

Bangor, Maine
PHILTRUM PRESS
1987

Signed title page, 1988.

MAY

26 MONDAY
Memorial Day

27 TUESDAY

28 WEDNESDAY

Marshall washes all these and more memories down with endless bottles of Shiner. When his wife finally dies, the man is overcome with the futility of life and the indignity of old age.

The Ideal, Genuine Man is a meditation on aging. The novel examines the life of a man. Not necessarily a good man, nor a bad one. Just a normal southern man with the usual prejudices and values. But Herman Marshall is also a powder keg with a rapidly burning fuse.

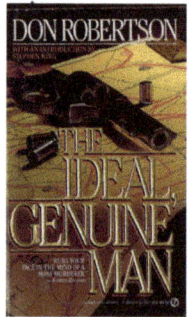

Signet
paperback
1989

This is a sad, profane, reflective story of a fading life. Until the final pages, when *The Ideal, Genuine Man* turns into the kind of nightmare Jack Ketchum might have dreamed up.

You've probably read a lot of books, but I doubt you've ever read anything like *The Ideal, Genuine Man*. It's a stunning novel. Just ask Stephen King. He not only admires the book, it is one of the very few publications from King's own Philtrum Press.

I have to make a note on the language in *The Ideal, Genuine Man*. It could never be done by a major publisher today. Sensitivity editors would drop dead. Herman Marshall is a man of his time, and his thoughts and vernacular are of his era. He isn't even hateful

MAY

29 THURSDAY

30 FRIDAY

31 SATURDAY

1 SUNDAY

---

about the words he uses. It's merely the way people thought and spoke then. Certainly, it was wrong, but we can't change the way people were. Nor was Don Robertson a hateful man. You only have to read *Praise the Human Season* or the *Morris Bird III* trilogy to see the humanity in his work. He was unflinchingly honest in his portrayals of people.

That wouldn't bother us, would it? We're horror fans. We go to the crucible to face hard truths every time we pick up a book or watch a movie.

– Mark Sieber,
horrordrive-in.com

Who is your favorite novelist of all time?

"Probably Don Robertson, author of *Paradise Falls, The Ideal, Genuine Man* and the marvelously titled *Miss Margaret Ridpath and the Dismantling of the Universe*. What I appreciate most in novels and novelists is generosity, a complete baring of the heart and mind, and Robertson always did that. He also wrote the best single line I've ever read in a novel: Of a funeral he wrote, "There were that day, o Lord, squadrons of birds."

– STEPHEN KING
The New York Times, June 4th, 2015

JUNE

_____
_____
_____
_____
_____
_____
_____
_____
_____
_____
_____
_____
_____
_____
_____
_____
_____
_____

BEST SEAT IN THE HOUSE

May 27th, 1993. Roxy Theater, Atlanta, Buckhead.

My introduction to Stephen King's work began later in my life than most other folks. It was back in 1984 when a co-worker clutched a hardcover copy of *IT* to her chest, like a Baptist going to church on Sunday. She read through it little by little, sharing with me what had scared the bejeezus out of her the previous night.

After lending me her copy, I was hooked and immediately dove into the archives and read everything I could get my hands on. Eventually I somehow discovered The Overlook Connection Bookstore, I think a friend had told me about this magical place where you can get your hands on all things King. I got my first copy of the Overlook Connection catalog and found a whole new world of fandom like I had never known. I became King obsessed. I simply HAD to have something more unique something signed, something rare, maybe even meeting the man one day?

JUNE

5 THURSDAY

6 FRIDAY

7 SATURDAY

8 SUNDAY

I became great friends with Dave Hinchberger at the Overlook. Here was a guy who not only had everything King you could imagine, but he had even met the man. Dave and I made a fast friendship.

We'd exchange notes and letters because the internet as we know it today was non-existent then. Soon we began casually conversing about the book biz and anything new about King (Dave was always known for having new tidbits on upcoming King things).

I think it was early on in 1993 that Dave let me know about this "thing" that was going to be happening in Atlanta. "Ed", Dave said "Steve's coming to Atlanta and this might be a good chance to see him".

I'm already totally in at this point, but yeah!, gimme some details.

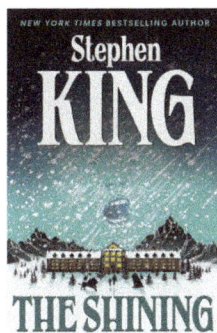

The Shining Vintage Trade Paperback 2013

JUNE

9 MONDAY

_____
_____
_____
_____
_____
_____
_____
_____
_____
_____
_____
_____
_____
_____
_____

10 TUESDAY

_____
_____
_____
_____
_____
_____
_____
_____
_____
_____
_____
_____
_____
_____
_____

11 WEDNESDAY

_____
_____
_____
_____
_____
_____
_____
_____
_____
_____
_____
_____
_____
_____
_____

Glenn Chadbourne, 2017.

Dave proceeded to tell me about THE ROCK BOTTOM REMAINERS band and show!

Omg, all those writers *and* rock and roll???

I'm in! Not only would I have a chance to (hopefully) SEE Stephen King and be in the same room as him, but I would finally meet my horror Sherpa guide who led me here, Dave.

I immediately booked vacation time at work, secured the grandparents to watch our three-year-old daughter and told my 5-month pregnant (then) wife that we were heading up to Atlanta to see Stephen King. The trip was long, remember the no-internet thing? The same goes for GPS. We lived by road signs and paper maps. Checked ourselves into a cheapie hotel once we got there and asked for directions to the Roxy theater.

I remember I was so excited to get there that I made my pregnant wife get ready early so we could get there early and be one of the first fans in line because I wanted a good seat up front. I don't know if you know this but pregnant women are not fans of standing in lines for any length of time.

It seemed like forever and finally the line started moving forward. We were in! I remember walking into the venue asking myself where all the seats were? No seats! Standing room only. Awesome… let's stand up front and get a good place to see "the King" and the band.

JUNE

12 THURSDAY

13 FRIDAY

14 SATURDAY
Flag Day

15 SUNDAY
Father's Day

My wife and I sat cross legged on the floor waiting. She's in *MISERY* (see what I did there?). I'm in my glory. Walking back up front to get us some refreshments, I see this larger-than-life gentleman dressed as good as any showman, talking to someone. I interrupted…

"Dave! Dave it's me Ed Yarb…"

"Fast Eddie! He replies (using my radio nickname, Dave's a huge fan of radio)

Dave doesn't shake hands he reaches out and pulls you in for a bear hug!

Now back into the show I cannot believe we have this kind of access to the stage. I walked up as the introduction s are made… Amy Tan, Dave Barry, blah blah blah… then finally, "and on guitar Mr. Steve King!" Spotlight on and the man walks out! There he is. He's real. He's moving around and I'm just a few feet away! Unreal. I can't tell you I remember a single song they played, I remember a surf anthem about a surfer lost at sea.

Well about three more songs go by and my wife is now swooning from pregnancy claustrophobia and… not feeling well, at all, and we have to go. All that planning, all that prep. Ugh!

But I can tell you I would do it all over again because Stephen King is a force to be around. There he was, large as life, right in front of me on stage. Best seats in the house I tell ya, best seats in the house.

I couldn't have done it without you Dave, even the half of *IT* I did get to do!

— Ed Yarb

Stephen King, *The Shining*. ABC TV. 1997
Warner Bros

JUNE

MONDAY   **TUESDAY**   **WEDNESDAY**

CUJO MEETS THE WOLVES

Living in New York, I've been close to a dozen Stephen King signings / events over the decades, but the one that stands out as the most memorable is the *Wolves of the Calla* event that took place at the Jacob Burns Film Center (formerly the Rome Theater) in Pleasantville, NY in the fall of 2003. The event consisted of a live interview of King conducted by New York Times literary critic Janet Maslin, audience Q&A, a screening of the film *Cujo*, and a meet and greet with Maslin and King.

Cujo theater poster,
Warner Bros. 1983

I arrived about 5 hours early, as I wanted to get a good seat in the theater (this was general admission, as with most Stephen King appearances). Amazingly, I was the first person there, and over the next 90 minutes, others began to arrive. A number of us were members of the pre-Facebook Internet group, SKEMERs, met up in line and got to know one another. About an hour before doors opened, King's limo arrived, and he and his companions parked down the road and we watched him enter a coffee shop to have breakfast. Everyone wanted to respect his privacy and I don't recall anyone breaking out of line to go pester him for an autograph or a selfie.

About 15 minutes before the venue opened, King and his group arrived at the theater. I was wearing a custom-made t-shirt featuring artwork from the first edition of

JUNE

19 THURSDAY
Juneteenth

_____
_____
_____
_____
_____
_____
_____
_____
_____
_____
_____
_____
_____
_____
_____
_____
_____

20 FRIDAY

_____
_____
_____
_____
_____
_____
_____
_____
_____
_____
_____
_____
_____
_____
_____
_____
_____

21 SATURDAY

_____
_____
_____
_____
_____
_____
_____
_____

22 SUNDAY

_____
_____
_____
_____
_____
_____
_____

The Stand and as King made his way to the theater entrance, he glanced at me and said, "Hey, cool shirt, man!" I could have gone home right then, and the day would have been worth it!

As we filed into the theater, each of us was given a small bag with a few goodies in it, including a paperback edition of *Cujo* and an event booklet.

Maslin was introduced and took the stage. She read a short and unnecessary bio of King, stumbling a few times, and King took the stage to a standing ovation. I could see that Maslin was a bit nervous, but King, clad in jeans and a t-shirt, very quickly put her at ease and as the interview progressed, King's informal down-to-earth and friendly disposition made the interview process flow naturally. His stories and answers to her questions were often humorous, and of course his continuing recovery from his somewhat recent accident (June 1999) was discussed at length.

After the interview, King took questions from the audience, most of which dealt with the remaining "Dark Tower" novels and King's slowly improving health. After the questions were answered, King joined the audience for the screening of *Cujo*. He sat about halfway back on the left side of the auditorium and cracked the audience up during the film by loudly speaking to the screen ("Don't get out of the car, lady!").

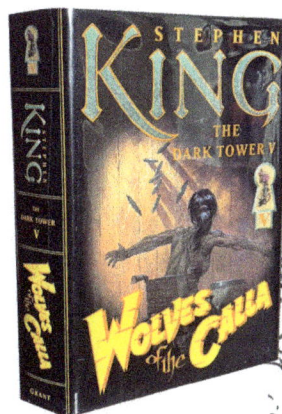

Dark Tower V: Wolves of the Calla,
Donald Grant 2003.

23 MONDAY · **24** TUESDAY · **25** WEDNESDAY

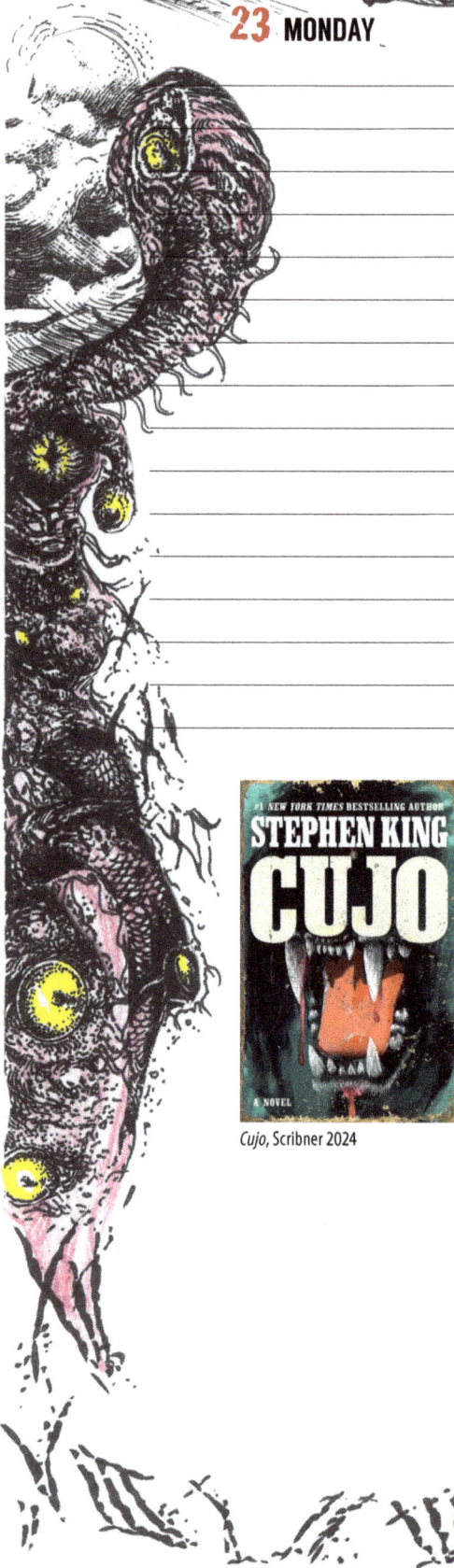

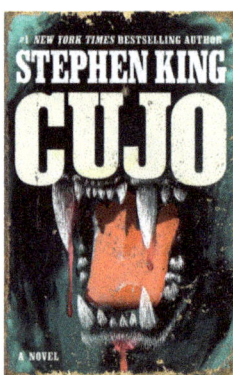

Cujo, Scribner 2024

It was surreal to be watching a King adaptation with him sitting a few rows away in a dark theater. It was undoubtedly a once-in-a-lifetime experience for everyone there!

As we filed out following the screening, a table was set up in the lobby with signed 2nd printing copies of *Wolves of the Calla*, and everyone received a copy. I recall feeling a bit bummed that the books were 2nd printings, but I ended up keeping my copy just to commemorate such a unique event. I did also buy a 1st printing, and to this day the signed copy is the only later printing of a book I own.

Subsequently, some of us were escorted upstairs for the meet and greet, which was a very causal affair with snacks and felt like a cocktail party. Some people got photos (I don't think my flip phone at the time took photos, and if it did, those are sadly long gone), we all chatted for a while, and then it was over.

There have been some interesting King signings over the years, but this one was the most memorable to me, especially due to the movie screening. I wish I had photos or a ticket stub to share with you all, but the best I can do is to share a pic of my signed DTV.

— Noah Mitchel

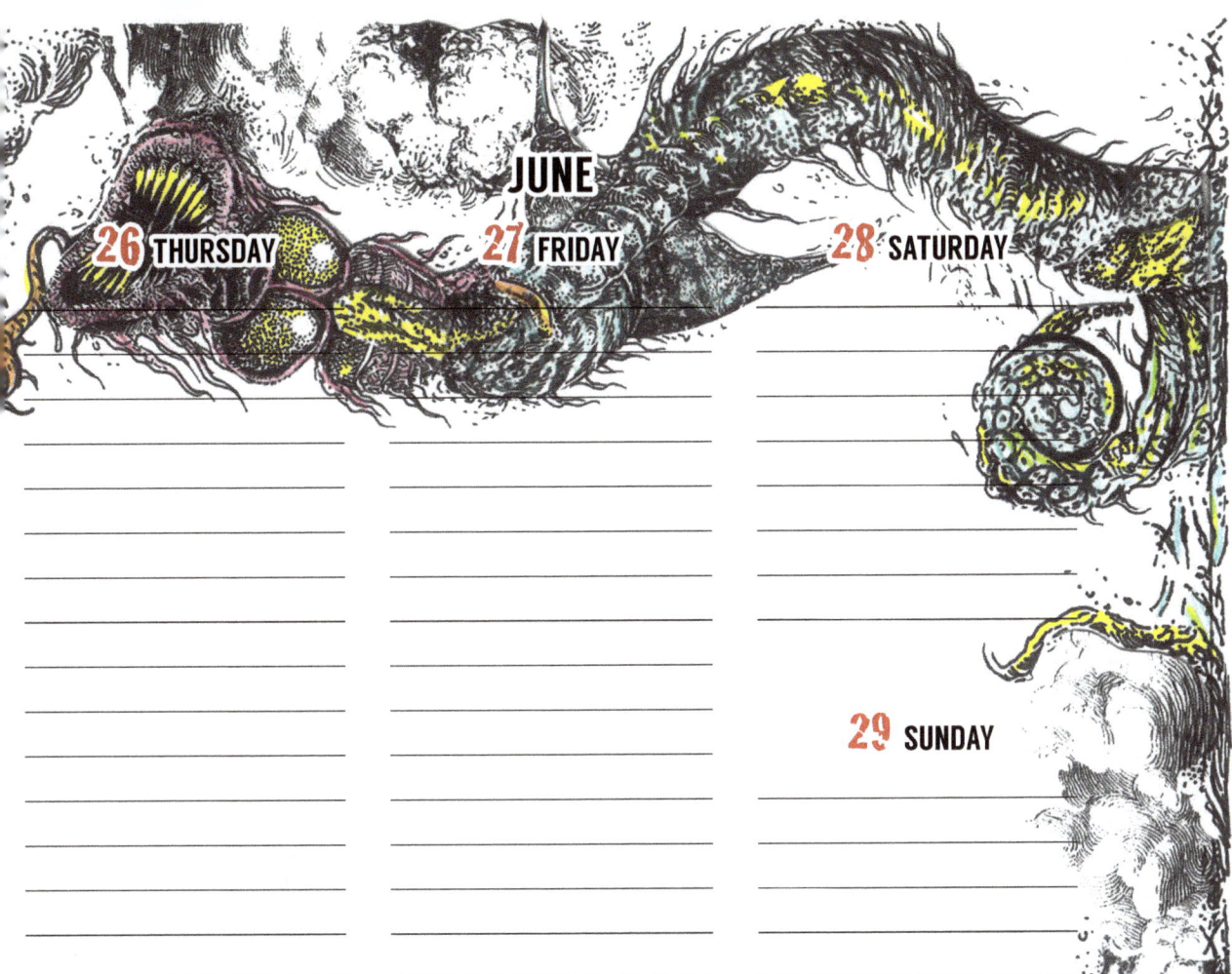

JUNE

26 THURSDAY

27 FRIDAY

28 SATURDAY

29 SUNDAY

"We have had the most bizarre Stephen King experiences…He is a totally normal person but some of his fans are lunatics. In front of him at a concert in Nashville one time was a woman waving back and forward with all 10 finger nails on fire."

– RIDLEY PEARSON, author, bass, vocals for the Rock Bottom Remainders

Glenn Chadbourne

30 MONDAY

1 TUESDAY

2 WEDNESDAY

DON'T SLEEP ON IT!

I want to begin by saying, if you are indecisive about doing something... buy that ticket! Book that flight!

In 2017 I attended a *Sleeping Beauties* book tour event at J. Scheidegger Center for the Arts at Lindenwood University, in St Charles, Mo. I was raised in Missouri, from the age of 8 -18.

I'm like a bumper sticker that I read once: "I wasn't born in Texas, but I got here fast as I could!"

I have family in Missouri, so my trip was not so costly. My niece, Kara and her boyfriend, Seth, and I attended the event together. We arrived in St. Charles very early, so we decided to grab a bite eat. But, first I suggested we do a drive by to see if there was a line forming yet. I told them if there was a line, to just drop me off and I would get in line. They could go eat, and bring me back something.

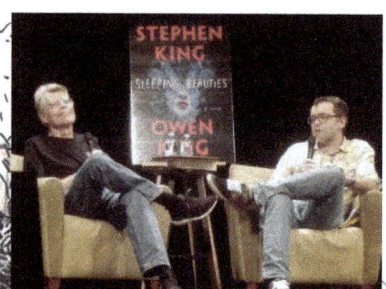

Photo: Marie Burns 2017

Yup!! There was a line formed already. We still ended up on the second row, center. While waiting in line, there was a reporter from the *St. Louis Post-Dispatch* interviewing attendees.

She stopped and talked to us, and I ended up in her article. So cool being mentioned in the same article as King. Every attendee received a copy of *Sleeping Beauties*. Only 400 attendees had a chance to receive a signed book. My niece and her boyfriend had already decided that if they got one, and I didn't, they would give it to me. It just so happened, we ALL three received one!

My only regret was not getting a photo of me with Stephen King in the background. My second trip to see him was a couple of years later. I traveled to Minnesota. Just so

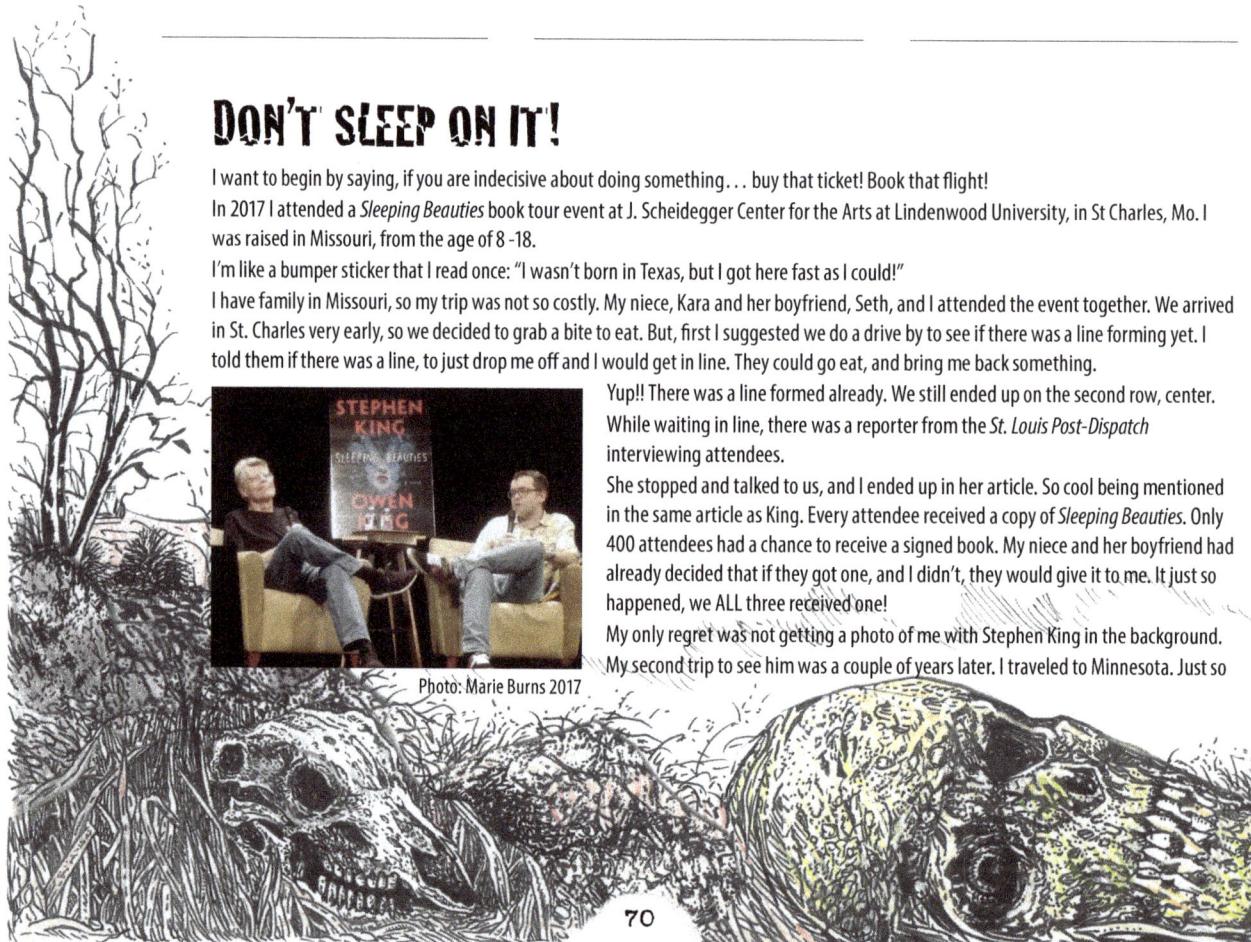

JULY

3 THURSDAY

_____
_____
_____
_____
_____
_____
_____
_____
_____
_____
_____
_____
_____
_____

4 FRIDAY
Independence Day

_____
_____
_____
_____
_____
_____
_____
_____
_____
_____
_____
_____
_____
_____

5 SATURDAY

_____
_____
_____
_____
_____
_____

6 SUNDAY

_____
_____
_____
_____
_____
_____
_____

happens, I have family in Minnesota. My cousin, Marina and I attended the events together. This trip was epic!

$116 round trip airfare. I know. I couldn't believe it either. I had to double check and make sure I booked it correctly. My cousin was a flight attendant, and she said it is cheap to fly from one big hub to another.

The Loft's WORDPLAY Opening Party featured The Rock Bottom Remainders at First Avenue.

The ticket for the concert was only $40. We got there early, and we were right up front. I got in early enough, that I was able to get Dave Barry to sign a CD that I had brought along, you know just in case!

They did a tribute to Prince, singing "KISS" while all dressed up in purple feather boas. Some staff members handed out some panties to the ladies up front, to toss onto stage. (Fyi, they still had tags.)

I waited until they were between songs. I sling shot mine at Stephen King's feet. He picked them up, raised his eyebrow, bit his bottom lip and nodded his head up and down. All while looking directly at me. Eeek! The closest I have come to meeting him. And being caught up in the moment, I still forgot to get a photo of me with him in the background!

The next day we went to a book festival to see him do an interview with Benjamin Percy.

Up front, again! The Wordplay Book Festival ticket was only $10. We were able to obtain a voucher to purchase a signed, *The Outsider* at book face value. That was their first annual book festival, so of course it was a learning curve for them. While in line to purchase the book, a woman was frustrated with how the line was organized. She asked if I wanted her voucher.

Well, you know the answer to that!

I was able to purchase not one, but two books! $60.00 for TWO signed Stephen King books.

Unheard of!! So, if I did the math right, my Minneapolis trip only cost $226.00. Enjoy life.

As Steve Jobs said, "The most important thing is to enjoy your life—to be happy—it's all that matters."

— Marie Burns

Photo: Marie Burns 2017

JULY

7 MONDAY

8 TUESDAY

9 WEDNESDAY

THE BIG SQUEEZE

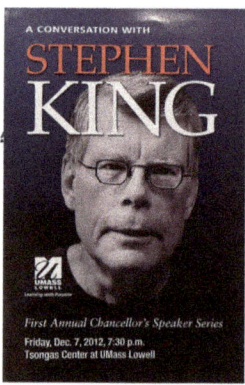

A CONVERSATION WITH
STEPHEN KING

First Annual Chancellor's Speaker Series
Friday, Dec. 7, 2012, 7:30 p.m.
Tsongas Center at UMass Lowell

University of Massachusetts
in Lowell 2012 poster

On Dec. 7, 2012, Stephen King gave a talk at the University of Massachusetts in Lowell. Tickets sold out quickly, but my sister, a generous alum of ULowell (as the school was once known), was able to get tickets to the talk AND the meet and greet reception beforehand.

The reception was crowded and Mr. King milled about the guests. A representative escorted me throughout the room, trying to get me close enough to meet Mr. King. Every time I seemed to be next in line to greet him, he asked for a Diet Coke and moved on. I eventually told my escort to stop trying to get me close because the frustration was ruining my evening. I decided to just focus on the talk I was about to hear. It was the best thing I could have done—the next thing I knew, someone was slipping a bracelet on my wrist, telling me not to show it to anyone and to go backstage after the talk for a photo opportunity!

JULY

10 THURSDAY

_____
_____
_____
_____
_____
_____
_____
_____
_____
_____
_____
_____
_____
_____
_____

11 FRIDAY

_____
_____
_____
_____
_____
_____
_____
_____
_____
_____
_____
_____
_____
_____
_____

12 SATURDAY

_____
_____
_____
_____
_____
_____
_____

13 SUNDAY

_____
_____
_____
_____
_____
_____
_____

I enjoyed a third-row seat, listening to Stephen King and author and professor Andre Dubus III have an entertaining and informative conversation. I was happy to be there and didn't think the evening could have been better.

After the talk, I went backstage with my sister. We were supposed to have a quick photo and move on but I brought my battered book club edition _Christine_—the first Stephen King book I ever read—and Mr. King was gracious enough to sign it. I was able to tell him the significance of the book and how great my sister was to get me tickets to the event. My sister and I still recall how tightly he squeezed us during the photo. My sister won a copy of _11/22/63_ that night, which she gifted to me.

Photo: Laurie Dupre 2012

The Stephen King Universe has continued to be very good to me. On 10/10/19, I attended An Evening With Joe Hill and Stephen King in Somerville, MA where they promoted _Full Throttle_ and _The Institute_ respectively. And in 2017 I had the opportunity to be an extra in Season One of _Castle Rock_.

— Laurie Dupre 10/8/24

i4 MONDAY   **i5** TUESDAY   **i6** WEDNESDAY

MY LIFE WITH THE REMAINDERS
or Why Didn't They Ask Dave Barry?

As the only non-writer in the band, I pleaded with the other Remainders to ghost-write this. "Forget it. You didn't let us lip-synch to Madonna tracks," they sang out in unison, slightly off-key. So, only the lonely...

In the fine rock & roll tradition, the Rock Bottom Remainders were conceived in a car. As a semi-pro musician with a day job in book publicity, I spend a lot of time driving touring authors around San Francisco. Some of them are so much fun to be with that conducting them from interview to interview doesn't feel like work. We'll start digging through my vast collection of tapes. I'll play weird food songs and they'll tell me about some Zairean Rockabilly group. Before I know it, another new friend is sitting in with my band, the Ray Price Club, at The

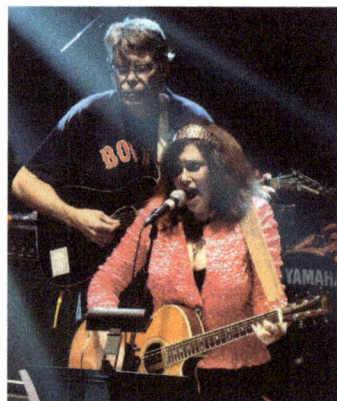

Kathi Kamen Goldmark and Stephen King

JULY

17 THURSDAY

18 FRIDAY

19 SATURDAY

20 SUNDAY

Blue Lamp. And he or she will get the sweetest, dreamiest look and tell me how lucky I am: "Writing is okay, but I was in a band in college and it was the most fun I ever had."

I decided to form a band of authors! We could burst upon the world at the 1992 American Booksellers Association convention in Anaheim!

As our debut approached, I became Remaindermom. Ridley Pearson, who plays in a real band and had some idea how bad we could be, made everyone a rehearsal tape. Amy Tan-with the help of a wig, shades, free weights and intensive karaoke work transformed herself into Ronnie Spector. Michael Dorris signed on as drummer, had to drop

Stranger Than Fiction CD. 1998 Don't Quit Your Day Job Records

JULY

21 MONDAY   **22** TUESDAY   **23** WEDNESDAY

_____   _____   _____
_____   _____   _____
_____   _____   _____
_____   _____   _____
_____   _____   _____
_____   _____   _____
_____   _____   _____
_____   _____   _____
_____   _____   _____
_____   _____   _____
_____   _____   _____
_____   _____   _____
_____   _____   _____
_____   _____   _____

out for personal reasons, then showed up at the gig to join us on percussion. Dave Barry agreed to play lead guitar if he could wear spandex; we made him wear it under his clothes. Barbara Kingsolver wrote from the Canary Islands to enlist on keyboards. Robert Fulghum's mandocello and folk background lent counterpoint to our headlong electricity.

Stephen King contributed rhythm guitar and an almost uncanny feel for teenage death songs. When Tad Bartimus came through town I invited her to join Amy and me in the Remainderettes.

THE ROCK BOTTOM REMAINDERS

All we lacked were loud frat-party types to sing "Louie Louie". The Critics' Chorus was born. Roy Blount, Matt Groening, Greil Marcus, Dave Marsh and Joel Selvin had all written books and rock criticism, and (even so) I felt they'd look good in Hawaiian shirts. Also, with all the critics in the band, who'd slam us? (I reckoned without Don Henley, who reviewed us so savagely as to make us feel almost serious.) Two ringers - pros Josh Kelly on drums and Jerry Peterson on sax - proved invaluably

JULY

24 THURSDAY

25 FRIDAY

26 SATURDAY

27 SUNDAY

instrumental. And Al Kooper, of Blues Project fame, volunteered to be musical director. He added laid-back zest, rock & roll cynicism, and a distinguished ear. He cut Roy's song.

After three days' rehearsal in a secret location - assisted by my co-workers Carole and Lorraine, a volunteer crew and "spousal units" led by Tabby King - we hit the Cowboy Boogie club's stage. When our audience of booksellers and publishers began to scream, dance and throw underwear, we felt more like rock stars than we'd dared to hope (except for

Amy Tan and Kathi Kamen Goldmark at The Electric Factory, April 22, 2010 Philadelphia

Marsh, whose standards are high). It was Fantasy Rock & Roll Camp. It raised money for the Homeless Writers' Coalition of Los Angeles, Literacy Volunteers of America and the Right To Rock Network, And we were so damn fine. In the words of emcee and weird food song collector Blount: "Ladies and Gentlemen, suspend your credibility for The ROCK...BOTTOM... RE-MAIN-DERS!"

— Kathi Kamen Goldmark (with secret help from Roy Blount Jr.)

28 MONDAY | **29** TUESDAY | **30** WEDNESDAY

GET A LEG UP!

I entered and won a competition run by the *Times* newspaper to get 2 x tickets to the Stephen King event at Battersea Park Events Arena, on Tuesday November 7, 2006 at 7.00 pm.

This was to be a talk and Q&A followed by a reading from *Lisey's Story*, and then a book signing by King.

At 1.00 pm on that day, King appeared at Borders Books and Music, Oxford Street, London for a book signing. He would sign for 2 hours only and each person was allowed two books to be signed. The books could be any book or whatever you wanted signed.

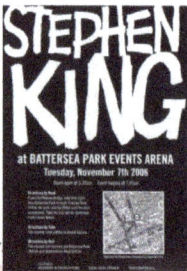

Problem. We live in the north of Scotland and would not be able to get to London in time to get a good place in the queue at Borders. I booked a hotel for me and my wife in Chelsea and a flight from Glasgow to London on the Tuesday morning.

I hit upon the idea of phoning up Borders Books and Music and telling them I was disabled and could they save me, and my wife a place in the queue.

I then looked out my medical boot and crutches which I still had from an accident, months previously. (I was fine now).

2006 Battersea flyer,
Hodder & Stoughton,
Waterstones

78

AUGUST

31 THURSDAY

_____
_____
_____
_____
_____
_____
_____
_____
_____
_____
_____
_____
_____
_____
_____

1 FRIDAY

_____
_____
_____
_____
_____
_____
_____
_____
_____
_____
_____
_____
_____
_____
_____

2 SATURDAY

_____
_____
_____
_____
_____
_____
_____

3 SUNDAY

_____
_____
_____
_____
_____
_____

On the Tuesday morning, we flew down to London and arrived a little late. We had to run along the packed streets of London with me in crutches to get to Borders on time. When we got to Borders we asked for the manager who then ushered us upstairs to the signing area. King was already signing books by then. The manager asked us to wait until he could get us in the queue. I was waiting very close to King and eventually the manager moved us into the queue. Nobody seemed to mind. If it was me, I would be furious at someone queue jumping, which is worse than murder in the UK.

Lisey's Story signing, Alan Kyle 2006, Battersea

Stephen King, Battersea Borders, London

I presented my mint copy of "Twice the Power" to King who exclaimed, "what is this?" Then, when he opened it at the title page, he recognized it as a _Needful Things_ proof. I got him to sign a copy of _Lisey's Story_ as well. My wife got her two books signed after I did. I managed to get a few photos of King signing some books while I was waiting.

stephen KING 'TWICE THE POWER' NEEDFUL THINGS FOUR PAST MIDNIGHT

'TWICE THE POWER'

Hodder & Stoughton

'TWICE THE POWER'

An exclusive presentation proof of the two new novels from the world's bestselling author

Stephen King

NEEDFUL THINGS – THE NEW HARDCOVER
FOUR PAST MIDNIGHT – THE NEW PAPERBACK

PUBLISHING
OCTOBER 4TH 1991

Hodder & Stoughton

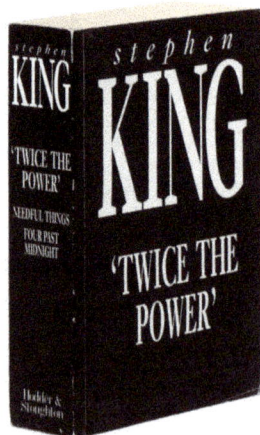

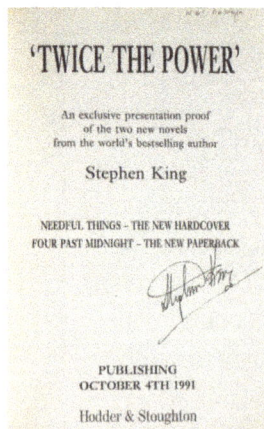

"Twice the Power"
Advance Proof,
Hodder & Stoughton
1991

After dinner, we made our way to the Battersea Park Events Arena where we noticed the *Lisey's Story* painted taxi. King did not arrive in that taxi. He had a limo. The taxi was just an advertisement. I had left my medical boot and crutches at the hotel as we had tickets for the event and plenty of time.

As competition winners we had good front and centre seats. The talk and Q&A was very good and King's reading was brilliant. He knows how to work an audience.

AUGUST

7 THURSDAY

8 FRIDAY

9 SATURDAY

10 SUNDAY

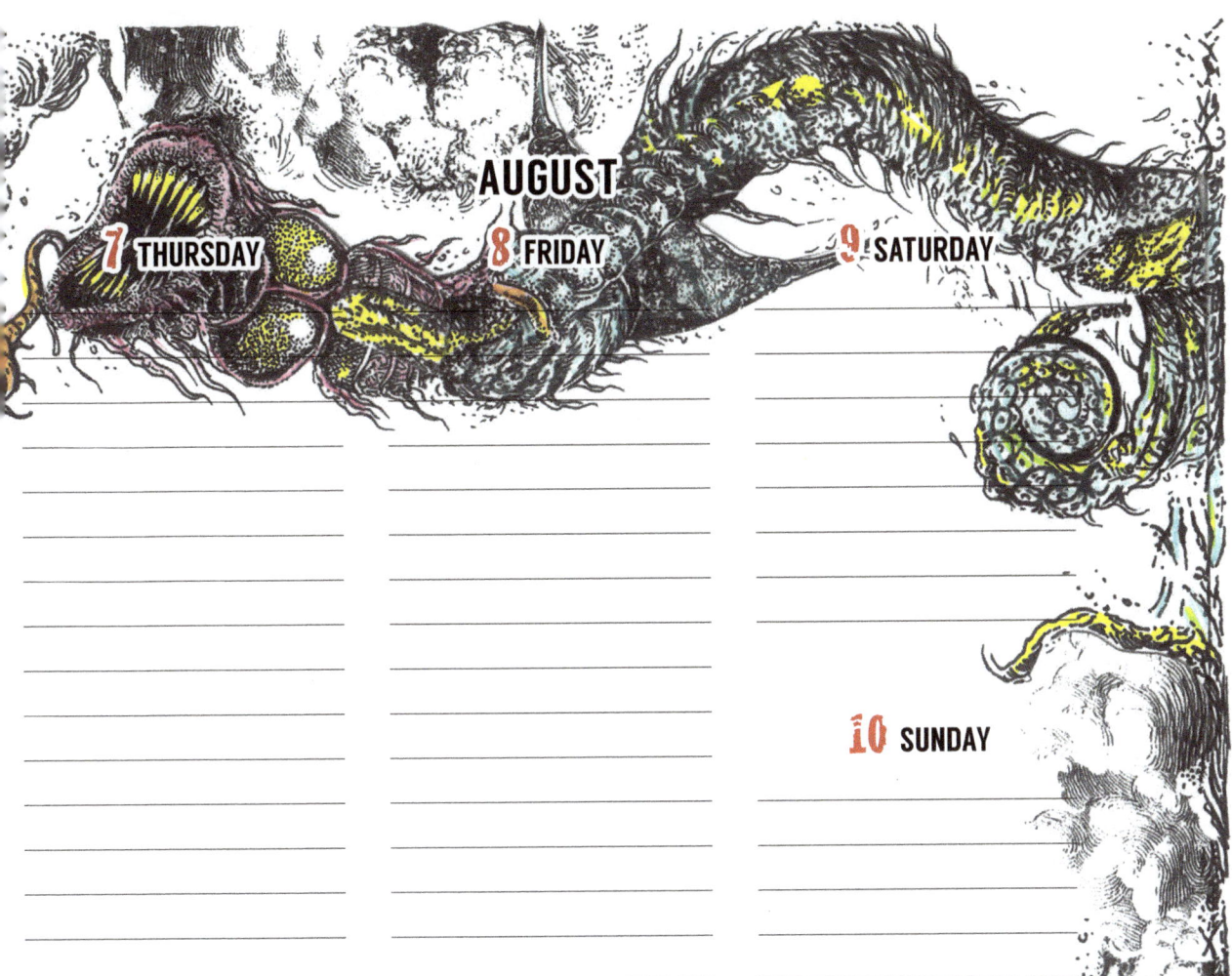

As he was finishing off his talk, a stampede for the signing area started. I spotted this happening and ran under the tape and bolted to the front. We ended up fifth in the queue with hundreds behind us. Once again King signed two books of any kind per person. I had brought a few unusual items and got them signed along with my wife's copies.

Promotional ad on a taxi for Stephen King's *Lisey's Story*, London, England 2006

On the way out we noticed a newspaper stand with dozens of *Times* newspaper supplements of King's visit to London and grabbed a few dozen for the other King fans we knew.

All together a great day out and between us we got eight rare King books signed. Some might say I was not very gentlemanly, but if you snooze… you lose.

— Alan Kyle (Mr. Rabbit Trick), United KIngdom

The Mist Limited Edition Lithograph Only 500 Signed Copies
17" x 11" Signed / Numbered by artist **Glenn Chadbourne**

Skeleton Crew: Unpublished Stephen King Anniversary Cover Lithograph Only 500 Signed
Copies 17" x 11" Signed / Numbered by artist **Pete Von Sholly**

Search for LITHOGRAPH at **StephenKingCatalog.com**

OVERLOOK CONNECTION PRESS   2023 Overlook Connection Press. Sent Rolled.

AUGUST

11 MONDAY

12 TUESDAY

13 WEDNESDAY

A SIGNING IN JERSEY

Back in the early 1990's, I had a sales rep at Doubleday press in New York City for many years. His name was Sam, a lovely fellow, and always a big help to our mail-order bookstore, The Overlook Connection. Of course, our main subject was their author Stephen King, as they had all the early years, the magic years some might call it, touting such releases as *Carrie*, *'Salem's Lot*, *The Stand*, *The Shining*, *Night Shift*, and *Pet Sematary*.

During one conversation, Sam told me that he was working at a Barnes and Noble bookstore in New Jersey and they hosted Stephen King for a signing. One of the attendees who stepped up to King, getting his book signed, crouched down on a knee to speak with Stephen King for a moment. As it turns out, it was Pat DiNizio, co-founder and songwriter of the band, The Smithereens. Pat was able to convince King to do an interview right then and there, with his portable cassette player. As Sam tells the story, the interview was about 15-20 minutes.

You see, I was in the music business for years, working for a decade at Polygram Records, and then a short stint at Relativity records before I went full-time as a bookstore and press. I

AUGUST

14 THURSDAY

15 FRIDAY

16 SATURDAY

17 SUNDAY

was also operating my mail-order bookstore of Stephen King on the side. Sam knew this and thought I'd appreciate this story. Ah, when music and books collide. With this information in mind, I thought I had a good chance to get in touch with Pat and see if he still had this interview. Here he was all over MTV, the radio, with their hits "A Girl Like You", "Blood and Roses", etc. and here I was trying to get a Stephen King interview, from the eighties, from the leader of The Smithereens.

Fast forward to the mid-nineties, I was in New York City with Relativity Records for a conference. The record executives, and I, we were headed to a recording studio to visit with one of our bands there. Our van pulled up out front, we exited, when right in front of me, coming out of the same studio... Pat DiNizio and The Smithereens!

I was introduced to Pat, and I immediately took the opportunity. "Pat, do you remember doing an interview with Stephen King at Barnes and Noble?"

He was quite surprised at this question. He said yes, he did do an interview with Stephen King at a book signing. His question to me was, "How did you know this? Were you there?"

I explained how I came into this information about the interview, and said I would be very interested in publishing it in one of our newsletters or in some other form.

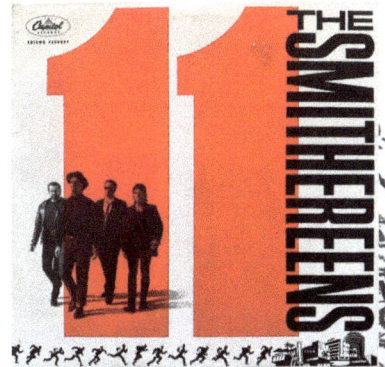

Smithereens 11, Capitol Records 1989

AUGUST

18 MONDAY

19 TUESDAY

20 WEDNESDAY

He said, "I do still have that cassette tape. It's buried in a bunch of stuff, but I will start looking for it because it would mean a lot for this to be published. Just the fact that anybody knows about this is amazing to me."

Email and the internet? Was not a thing yet, so Pat and I exchanged a couple of letters and we spoke on the phone. He said he'd been performing these living room concerts, and he'll eventually have one in Atlanta and he would give me a call, and keep the discussion going, especially talking about Stephen King's work. Maybe in all this he'd run across this "misplaced" Stephen King interview.

So, time marched on, I began working full-time on my bookstore and publishing and things trailed off, as they do. Life takes over when you're raising a family, working on the business, etc. every corner filled. Such is life.

It occurred to me, many years later, that I had never heard from Pat about that Atlanta living room concert. I just assumed he had stopped performing those concerts and never made it to town. So, I started looking for information about him (now that the internet was here and all-knowing), and the band and

AUGUST

24 SUNDAY

what was currently happening, so we could possibly reengage on this Stephen King interview. After all these years he may have found it!

It was not to be. It turns out I was too late. Pat had passed away, not more than six months previously, in 2017, at age 62. My heart sunk. I'm 62 as I write this and as far as I'm concerned I'm going to be around as long as the universe lets me. That was too young. I'm very sorry he's gone.

And, we'll never discover this lost Stephen King interview by Pat, which may still be sitting in some box, in some closet, or storage, somewhere with his family in New Jersey, where he lived. I just want to say thanks to Pat, wherever he's landed in the universe, for at least trying and taking the time with me on this. I wish I could tell Sam, who, unbeknownst to him, began this adventure and how we had a chance meeting. We haven't been in touch in decades.

I can just imagine the smile Sam would be wearing if he ever heard that I'd made contact.

Pat was obviously a big fan of Stephen King. I'll never forget when I mentioned the interview to him, there on that sidewalk in sunny July, in New York City, his face beamed, came alight, his eyes widened and he said...

... "Yeah, I'm a huge Stephen King fan."

– Dave Hinchberger

Doubleday

AUGUST

25 MONDAY	**26** TUESDAY	**27** WEDNESDAY
_____	_____	_____
_____	_____	_____
_____	_____	_____
_____	_____	_____
_____	_____	_____
_____	_____	_____
_____	_____	_____
_____	_____	_____
_____	_____	_____
_____	_____	_____
_____	_____	_____
_____	_____	_____
_____	_____	_____
_____	_____	_____

BEST BIRTHDAY, EVER!

I heard Stephen and Owen King were going out on a book tour for _Sleeping Beauties_. My son said he would buy the tickets for me for my birthday. So, I started looking for tickets. Sold out! But I found 2 tickets on Craigslist! They were $50 each and that included a hard cover copy of _Sleeping Beauties_ and random copies were autographed by Stephen and Owen King.*

My son Nathan, my youngest daughter Breanna, and I planned our trip for September 27, 2017 to Annandale-on-Hudson (New York). This was the day after my oldest daughter's birthday, Chelsea (sorry couldn't forget her in my story). The signing is a little over 4 hours away from my home in Dekalb Junction, New York. My husband Matt always did the driving but he couldn't go so it was up to me.

Nathan and I were going to go to the event and Breanna was going to be our "getaway driver". She was going to drop us off and pick us up so we could avoid the long line of traffic.

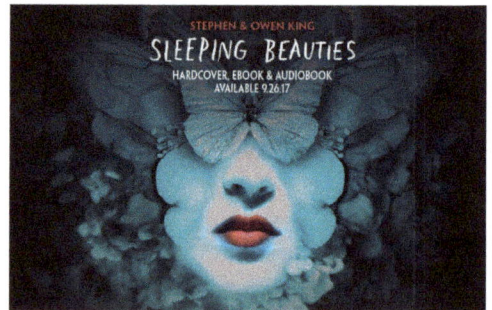

STEPHEN & OWEN KING
SLEEPING BEAUTIES
HARDCOVER, EBOOK & AUDIOBOOK
AVAILABLE 9.26.17

AUGUST

28 THURSDAY

29 FRIDAY

30 SATURDAY

31 SUNDAY

I was very nervous that I was going to get all the way there and the person I bought the tickets from was not going to be there but I had to take the chance. I had always wanted to meet Stephen King in person and this was my best shot.

On the day of the event the 3 of us headed out. My vehicles' air conditioner decided not to work but we made a quick stop at the auto parts store for a recharge and we were good to go.

We arrived at our destination early so we stopped at a pizza place for dinner. Then we headed to the venue. I messaged my ticket seller and we met to complete our transaction. As luck would have it they had an extra ticket which I bought for my daughter. This ticket put me just 5 rows from Stephen King! OMG! We were not allowed to take pictures or record during the event.

SOLD OUT!
Event date:
Wednesday, September 27, 2017 - 7:00pm
Event address:
Fisher Center for the Performing Arts at Bard,
60 Manor Ave, Annandale-on-Hudson, NY 12504
Presented by Oblong Books & Music and
the Richard B. Fisher Center for the Performing
Arts at Bard College
Tickets: $40
includes one copy of SLEEPING BEAUTIES*

SEPTEMBER

1 MONDAY *Labor Day*	**2 TUESDAY**	**3 WEDNESDAY**

However I did sneak a pic of my seat and my kid's seats before the show. Breanna snuck a pic of me and I had a smile from ear to ear but I can't find it.

So here is where it gets good. Stephen and Owen came on stage and they allowed questions from the audience. I raised my hand and I was the first person picked. Eeeeek! So, you may be asking yourself what did I ask Mr. King? Most people ask him about his writing and where he gets his ideas from, but not me. I asked him why he doesn't bring Molly, a.k.a. "the thing of evil," on tour? This was after I told him he was awesome or something fan girlish like that. His response, after he told everyone who Molly was, he said "she would get all of the attention." For maybe a minute I had his full undivided attention and at that moment there was only 2 people in the room, not 800. I didn't think I would ever stop smiling.

But wait it gets even better.

So we finished the event and on the way

Stephen and Owen King, Bards College, Photo John Meore 2017

SEPTEMBER

4 THURSDAY

_____
_____
_____
_____
_____
_____
_____
_____
_____
_____
_____
_____
_____
_____
_____
_____
_____
_____
_____

5 FRIDAY

_____
_____
_____
_____
_____
_____
_____
_____
_____
_____
_____
_____
_____
_____
_____
_____
_____
_____
_____

6 SATURDAY

_____
_____
_____
_____
_____
_____
_____
_____

7 SUNDAY

_____
_____
_____
_____
_____
_____
_____
_____

out we got to grab our books. My son, my daughter and I all grabbed one and peeked to see if we were one of the lucky ones to get an autographed copy. No, no and no. So, I was of course disappointed but still on a high from my encounter with the great one.

We make our way to the car to head home. All-of-a-sudden I thought, would my kids know to look at several of the pages? They did not. So, we all checked again.

Then, my daughter says OMFG! It's signed! Its signed!

She hands it to me, and it is in fact signed. Then she gives it to me says "happy birthday Mom."

One of my best days ever.

        – Beverly Robinson, New York.

*As a special bonus, a limited number of attendees will randomly receive a signed copy / This event includes an audience Q&A but will not include a public book signing.

SLEEPING BEAUTIES

Glenn Chadbourne

8 MONDAY   **9** TUESDAY   **10** WEDNESDAY

Don't Play So Loud: 2004 Wannapalooza Tour

A note from Dave Barry and the Rock Bottom Remainders:

Teacher Man by Frank McCourt. Scribner 2005

"The World Famous (in certain places) Rock Bottom Remainders are getting ready to rock the Midwest this October. We're going on a four-city tour that will take us to St. Louis, the Rock and Roll Hall of Fame in Cleveland, the House of Blues in Chicago, and Detroit. We'll be traveling by bus, just like real rock stars, except of course that many real rock stars have actual talent. We may not have that, but we DO have a bunch of famous authors, including Amy Tan, Mitch Albom, Ridley Pearson, Scott Turow, Greg Iles, Roy Blount, Jr., and Kathi Kamen Goldmark, who founded the band. And – for the first time – Frank "The Harmonica King" McCourt.

Also performing with us once again will be Roger McGuinn, legendary co-founder of the Byrds, who really DOES have talent,

SEPTEMBER

11 THURSDAY

12 FRIDAY

13 SATURDAY

14 SUNDAY

and who has been giving the band valuable musical tips to improve our sound, such as "Don't play so loud."

We are going to rock the nation's Heartland so hard that there could be bruising as far away as the nation's Spleenland, and possibly even the nation's Kidneyland.

It's all for a great cause. So, get your tickets now, and tell your friends. If you have no friends, make some, because they will not want to miss this event."

— Dave Barry, Lead Guitar, Vocals

And Roger McGuinn says…. "Touring with the Rock Bottom Remainders has been a blast! This will be my 4th tour with them. Dave Barry has always said that touring with them would surely ruin my career, but so far it's hard to tell if that's true. Maybe it takes a while."

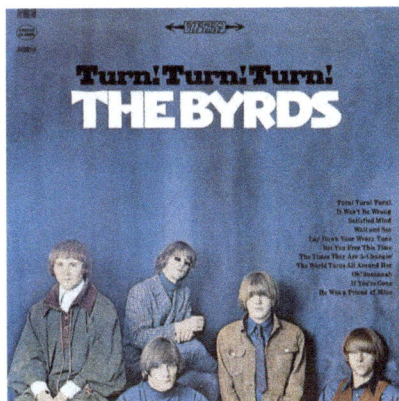

The Byrds *Turn Turn Turn*, Columbia 1965

93

SEPTEMBER

15 MONDAY

16 TUESDAY

17 WEDNESDAY

RESPECT!

Where did the Rock Bottom Remainders perform their first show?

What does Aretha Franklin and the Rock Bottom Remainders have in common?

The Rock Bottom Remainders gave their tours a title. Can you name any of them?

During their 2004 tour what unique item did they auction off at each venue? Only one per venue.

ABA
AMERICAN BOOKSELLERS ASSOCIATION

SEPTEMBER

18 THURSDAY

_____
_____
_____
_____
_____
_____
_____
_____
_____
_____
_____
_____
_____
_____

19 FRIDAY

_____
_____
_____
_____
_____
_____
_____
_____
_____
_____
_____
_____
_____
_____

20 SATURDAY

_____
_____
_____
_____
_____
_____

21 SUNDAY

_____
_____
_____
_____
_____
_____

Answers:

A1: Premiered at the American Booksellers Association trade show in Anaheim, California, 1992.

A2: The Rock Bottom Remainders used the tour bus that was previously Aretha Franklin's.

A3: **WannaPalooza 2004** October 26-30 covered, St. Louis – Chicago – Cleveland – Detroit.

Wordstock 2010 tour includes gigs on April 20–24 in several East Coast cities, April 20-21: Washington D.C., April 21: The 9:30 Club, April 22: Philadelphia, Electric Factory April 22: New York, Nokia Theatre, April 24: Boston, The Royale.

The Past Our Bedtime tour June 22nd, 2012, A Tour in honor of former bandmate Kathi Goldmark had two shows. The 22nd was at the El Rey Theater, Los Angeles. The June 23rd concert in Anaheim is at the American Library Association conference and open to registered attendees only.

A4: A guitar signed by everyone in the band was auctioned off at each concert.

Signed King guitar, Raptis Rare Books, raptisrarebooks.com

95

SEPTEMBER

22 MONDAY

23 TUESDAY
Rosh Hashanah

24 WEDNESDAY

IS STEPHEN KING... WORTH IT?

I discovered this question on the internet from 2014 about seeing Stephen King in person. This was for his six-city tour for his then new release, *Revival*. The tour began in New York City and continued through Washington DC, Kansas City, Wichita, Austin, and South Portland.

Have any of you been to a Stephen King book signing/event? Is it worth it?

He's coming to my city soon. Tickets are $30. That gets you in the door, and a first edition hard copy of his new book (*Revival*). Signed copies will be distributed randomly, so no guarantees. Have any of you done it? Is it worth the price of admission?

— thearmadillo, reddit

SEPTEMBER

25 THURSDAY

26 FRIDAY

27 SATURDAY

28 SUNDAY

RESPONSES:

Dude, it's Stephen King! Do it! – Account deleted, reddit

"Yes, it's worth it. I've seen him twice. The first time was at a signing to promote *Four Past Midnight*, and I had to stand in line for three hours. Even after all that time, he was as nice as could be when my turn came to get my books signed. The second time I saw him was during his motorcycle tour for *Insomnia*. He spoke to a packed house for 90 minutes, and was incredibly entertaining. So, do it!

Thirty dollars is a deal." – dwenglish, reddit

"I stood in line (overnight! was #36 in line) to see Stephen King when he was doing his book tour for *Under the Dome*. Didn't cost me a cent to see him either. However, they did not allow anyone to bring any books to have signed other than *Under the Dome*, and it was required that you purchase the book at the store where he did the signing.

I would not have traded the experience of seeing one of my favorite authors in person for anything though. Even though I was up all night, the people in the line were super nice! One person brought hot chocolate, and someone else had several trays of mini cupcakes to share. Definitely go, if you have a chance to see ANY author in person! Especially Stephen King."

– Sms231, reddit

Glenn Chadbourne

SEPTEMBER

"MY FIRST STADIUM AUDIENCE!"

– Stephen King, UMass at Lowell

Stephen King took the stage at UMass at Lowell, December 7, 2012 to a packed at the Tsongas Center there. "A Conversation with Stephen King" was moderated by Andre Dubus III, best-selling author, and professor

Stephen King at Umass 12-7-2012

in UMass Lowell's English Department. There were thousands in attendance at the Tsongas Center which can seat 6,496. Floor seats were $50 and general admission in the stands was $30. Admission was free to UMass students who applied for a ticket. Stephen King also held a special master class for UMass Lowell creative writing majors during his visit to the university. Five dollars of every ticket was donated to help endow a new scholarship fund in his and his wife, Tabitha's name.

King's appearance marked the debut of the new UMass Lowell Chancellor's Speaker Series, which later featured Oprah Winfrey and Meryl Streep.

Stephen King took questions from the audience after his talk. Here's a couple I thought were memorable:

OCTOBER

2 THURSDAY
Yom Kippur

3 FRIDAY

4 SATURDAY

5 SUNDAY

Signing one of two chairs auctioned off at the event.

A young man walks up to the microphone:
"Hi, hi, I'm talking to Stephen King!" The crowd laughs.

SK: "How old are you?"

YM: "I'm eleven-years old."

SK: "You go on with your bad self! What's your question?"

YM: "What was one of your best writing moments when you had your best idea and it just came to you?"

Stephen King at Umass 12-7-2012. Signing one of two chairs auctioned off at the event.

SK: "Oh man, what a great question that is. There have been a lot of times, you know, the thing is, I'm so lucky to be able to do this. Because you know, the thing is, like there are certain people in life where everybody else says we have to grow up, you stay a kid and play in

OCTOBER

6 MONDAY **7 TUESDAY** **8 WEDNESDAY**

_____ _____ _____
_____ _____ _____
_____ _____ _____
_____ _____ _____
_____ _____ _____
_____ _____ _____
_____ _____ _____
_____ _____ _____
_____ _____ _____
_____ _____ _____
_____ _____ _____
_____ _____ _____
_____ _____ _____
_____ _____ _____

Stephen King at Umass 12-7-2012

the playground. You'll be our designated playground person. You go play and we'll enjoy what it is that you do. The best idea in some ways, this is terrible to say, but I was in Boulder, Colorado, and I was driving on the Boulder Denver cut off from 36, and I was listening to a radio station in Arvada. It was one of these Bible shouters (crowd laughs) I love those guys, no I do seriously love those guys, I love the cadence of them, you know, it's a beautiful thing. And this guy was talking about some Old Testament book, and he's saying, 'once in every generation, the plague shall fall among them.' And we were living near a chemical warfare dump in that area, and there was a lot of talk about it, and I thought, what if there was a plague, and it killed just about everybody, and there were only a few people left? I thought to myself I'm going to write that and that was just such a blast, and it turned into *The Stand*, and it was good."

Then the next audience member steps up to the mic and says:

"Hi, my name's Diane. Three of my favorite things are reading, the Red Sox, and one of the best authors I've ever had the pleasure and privilege of reading, Stephen King. I happen to have a picture here of all

OCTOBER

9 THURSDAY

10 FRIDAY

11 SATURDAY

12 SUNDAY

three of these, which is a very young Stephen King, leaning against the wall of a vomitorium in Fenway Park, reading a book. I'm wondering if you remember what book you were reading in this picture."

SK: "Hand it down here." The picture-poster was handed up to Stephen King and moderator Andre Dubus III both examined the photo to take a closer look. The audience starts yelling for them to "turn it over," which they do and see the words "please sign this" written in large letters. Stephen King promptly pulls out a pen and signs the poster, while the audience applauds in unison at his generosity. Andre

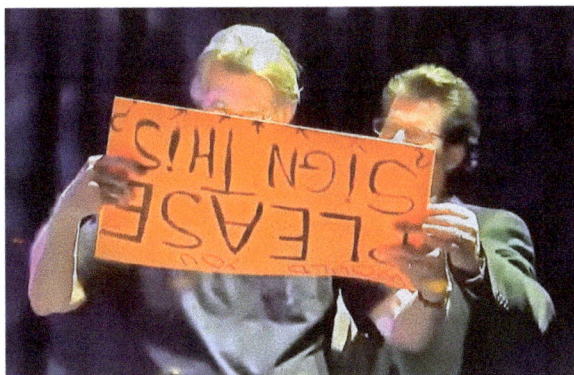

Stephen King and Andre Dubois III at Umass 12-7-2012

Dubus III takes the poster back down to Diane and says "you're wicked smahht!" while Diane does a dance holding the poster above her head, running down the aisle. I agree, she was a genius, she was "smahht!"

Do you know this photo of Stephen King at Fenway Park, reading a book? What is the book?

Stephen and Andre answer together:

SK: "It's The Friends of Eddie Coyle by George V. Higgins."

OCTOBER

13 MONDAY
Columbus Day
Indigenous Peoples' Day

14 TUESDAY

15 WEDNESDAY

NIRVANA

Stephen King premiered a new short story by reading it to a sold-out audience of over 6,000 at UMass in Lowell Massachusetts in 2012. What is the name of this story?

Where did it first appear in print?

It eventually appeared in Stephen King's own book. What title?

What was the genesis of this story?

Artwork by
Glenn Chadbourne

OCTOBER

16 THURSDAY

_____
_____
_____
_____
_____
_____
_____
_____
_____
_____
_____
_____
_____
_____
_____

17 FRIDAY

_____
_____
_____
_____
_____
_____
_____
_____
_____
_____
_____
_____
_____
_____
_____

18 SATURDAY

_____
_____
_____
_____
_____
_____
_____
_____

19 SUNDAY

_____
_____
_____
_____
_____
_____

Answers:

A1: "Afterlife"

A2: First published in the June 2013 edition of *Tin House*, an American literary magazine and publisher.

A3: *The Bazaar of Bad Dreams: Stories*.

A4: The story was later collected and re-introduced in the November 3, 2015 anthology *The Bazaar of Bad Dreams*, in which King revealed that the idea came from his own musings on mortality as he grew older.

Artwork by Glenn Chadbourne
From the New Stephen King Cover Series No. 9
Available from StephenKingCatalog.com

_____
_____
_____
_____
_____
_____
_____
_____
_____
_____
_____
_____
_____
_____
_____
_____
_____
_____

STEPHEN KING GAVE US A PEAK, UNDER THE DOME!

Stephen King was on tour to promote his newest book *Under the Dome*. It was his only stop in Canada at the Canon Theatre in Toronto, Ontario on November 19, 2009. My wife Bonita and I were on vacation and we decided to attend the event that night.

It was a beautiful fall evening in Toronto and the Canon theatre was packed, sold out, for an up close and personal interview and discussion with Stephen King. Moderated by Canadian film director David Cronenberg, who brought King's *The Dead Zone* to the big screen back in 1983. Stephen King was introduced by George Stroumboulopoulos.

Upon entering the Canon Theatre, you could obtain colored tickets with a chance of being selected to take home a signed event copy of the novel, signed by Stephen King, drawn at the end of the night. I was lucky enough to be one of the two hundred people who obtained a signed copy of the book to save as a keepsake from the event.

I still remember how amazed Stephen King was as he walked out to the center of the stage and panned the audience. He could not

Under the Dome tour, Canada. Jason Brenton, 2009

The Canon Theatre
244 Victoria Street, Toronto
AN EVENING WITH
Stephen King
Thu Nov 19, 2009 8:00PM
ORCH N 3 $28.00
Order #2276119
GST (R1999-23325) @ $3.00 CIF Included

OCTOBER

23 THURSDAY   **24** FRIDAY   **25** SATURDAY

26 SUNDAY

believe the number of people in the audience and the first words out of his mouth was "Holy Shit." He claimed it was the largest audience that he had ever addressed at a book event.*

Stephen read the first chapter of his new novel, *Under the Dome*, and he discussed several of his older works. He then continued discussing *Under the Dome*. Every time he mentioned a title of one of his books the crowd cheered, and he seemed to get a charge out of it and continued to do it throughout the remainder of the event.

YouTube video, King & Cronenberg 2009

One of the highlights from the event was the announcing of a possible new book to follow up on *The Shining* called *Doctor Sleep*. The follow up book would focus on Danny Torrence, now in his forties as an orderly traumatized by the childhood events depicted in the first novel.

It was an amazing evening and a night that I will never forget for the rest of my life. If you ever get a chance to see King in person I highly recommend it.

— Jason Brenton, Canada

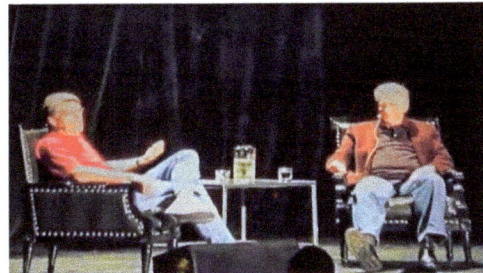

*The Canon theater seating capacity is 2,300.

105

OCTOBER

27 MONDAY

28 TUESDAY

29 WEDNESDAY

PLEASE. . . DON'T SIGN THE BOOKS

Stephen King, even on his early tours, I'm sure never received this request from a bookstore. In fact, I'd never heard of a situation like this before I ran across this story. Did you know that the author of *The Exorcist*, William Peter Blatty, was requested not to sign his books?

The Exorcist, a cross stitch

The beginnings of how *The Exorcist* came to be published happened at a party. William Peter Blatty, already an established screenwriter with films *A Shot in the Dark* with Peter Sellers, and *Darling Lili* with Julie Andrews, among others. His manuscript for *The Exorcist*, a retelling of a supposed exorcism from 1949, of a young boy, and the desperate family trying to get help. He'd discovered this story while attending Georgetown University. Blatty wasn't getting any takers.

While attending a party in 1968, he met Max Jeff, an editor for Bantam books, who asked what he was working on (like any good publisher would), and Blatty told him. The editor said he'd publish it

106

OCTOBER

30 THURSDAY

_____
_____
_____
_____
_____
_____
_____
_____
_____
_____
_____
_____
_____
_____

31 FRIDAY
Halloween

_____
_____
_____
_____
_____
_____
_____
_____
_____
_____
_____
_____
_____
_____

1 SATURDAY

_____
_____
_____
_____
_____
_____

2 SUNDAY
Day of the Dead
Daylight Saving Time End

_____
_____
_____
_____
_____

and paid him a $25,000 advance. That chance meeting was a stroke of luck for *The Exorcist*. *The Exorcist* became a book that to date has sold over 13 million copies in the USA alone have been translated into over a dozen languages.

In the beginning it hardly sold a copy. When Blatty was on his initial book tour, nobody was buying the book. Nobody. So, when he would go into the bookstores, the managers would ask if he wouldn't sign any of the unsold books, because if you sign them, they can't return them to the publisher. That must have been crushing.

He went back to New York City, visiting with his agent at the Four Seasons Hotel. Then the Dick Cavett show called and had an immediate open slot and asked if he'd be a guest. Apparently Robert Shaw, who was starring in *Jaws* at the time, was in the green room and couldn't go on. Blatty ran six blocks to the studio. Dick Cavett said he hadn't read the book, wasn't religious, and had Blatty tell him about *The Exorcist*. William Blatty had forty minutes to talk about *The Exorcist*, and the following week it went to number one on the New York Times bestseller list, and from there it began a history making run from book to film.

I wonder how many did get an *Exorcist book* signed back then.

William Peter Blatty passed away, January 12th, 2017.

"RIP William Peter Blatty, who wrote the great horror novel of our time. So long, Old Bill."

— Stephen King, Twitter

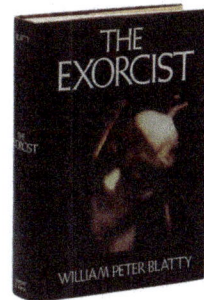

The Exorcist
First Print Hardcover
Harper & Row, New York, 1971

NOVEMBER

MILK, BREAD... STEPHEN KING!... CHECK!

Yes, I met Stephen King at Tesco* store, Lakeside, Essex, England. during the *Lisey's Story* promotion tour.

King photo,
Cliff Masters
2006.

A few weeks before, I was grocery shopping there and I noticed a poster for *Lisey's Story*. Being a Constant Reader it immediately had my attention. I could not believe my eyes, my favourite author was coming to my local supermarket!!!

The week before I spent planning what I would

108

NOVEMBER

6 THURSDAY   **7** FRIDAY   **8** SATURDAY

9 SUNDAY

say to him during those few golden seconds and I settled on "you're like a best friend I've never met" (I know, I know).

As we queued we were told "don't speak to him."

The hell with that and I took my opportunity.

Stephen replied "Thanks, how you doing fella?"

And it was over. . . just like that!

TESCO

A brief encounter to be forever cherished and never forgotten.
I have attached my photo just to show that I didn't dream this wonderful day!
— Cliff Masters, England

*TESCO has over 5,000 stores, mostly in the UK, and other countries. TESCO's superstores in the UK are comparable to the Walmart superstores in the US.

NOVEMBER

10 MONDAY

11 TUESDAY
Veterans Day

12 WEDNESDAY

Only 200 posters printed of the Rock Bottom Remainders
1998 Bangor, Maine appearance

ROCK BOTTOM BANGOR

Report from the Rock Bottom Remainders' Concert, May 8th, 1998

A dense fog hangs in the air of the Bangor Auditorium. Those in the audience may be inclined to first think of Stephen King's "The Mist," or perhaps of the remnants of one of Dave Barry's exploding animals. Then, a jet of the stuff spurts from a machine behind the well-equipped concert stage, and the audience forgets for a moment the literary aspects of the evening. That's a fog machine, those are real instruments, and this, just maybe, will be a real concert.

Suddenly, the house lights go down, and a spotlight from behind picks out the form of Roy Blount, Jr., a member of the Critic's Chorus section of the Remainders, who doubles as emcee for the band. In a clipped Southern accent burbling with good humor, he announces the members of the band as they appear on stage.

First up is Dave Barry, an immensely funny humor columnist, at present wearing a T-shirt which reads Poupon U. He explains, "It's from a mustard company!" As usual, Dave is two jokes ahead of the rest of us. He's also on lead guitar, strumming and tuning away.

In rapid succession, Roy brings out the rest of the Critic's Chorus. Joel Selvin ("If you rearrange the letters of his last name it almost spells 'Elvis!'"), Dave Marsh (who has become a cross-dressing legend amongst the band) and two locals: Joni Averill of the Bangor Daily News and Ric Taylor, meteorologist for WVII-TV in Bangor.

Another Maineiac (and part of the Remainderettes this evening), the multitalented Tess Gerritsen, who not only writes medical thrillers and is an actual medical doctor (Stephen King: "She's the only one of us who can prescribe Viagra!"), but also plays a mean electric violin. Rounding out the Remainderettes are Amy Tan, a well-respected author specializing in multigenerational family novels (seen now in leopard

110

NOVEMBER

13 THURSDAY

14 FRIDAY

15 SATURDAY

16 SUNDAY

skin and leather), and Kathi Goldmark, the "Band Mom" and media escort who began the Remainders and have been with them every step of the way.

Two band members have had some previous musical experience: radio host Mitch Albom (author of *Tuesdays with Morrie* and Elvis Presley impersonator) and Ridley Pearson (author of *Undercurrents* and Buddy Holly channeler) lend vocals and guitars to this already crowded lineup.

In a coup of stunt casting, the group has wrangled Warren Zevon, an actual rock and roll guy who's had songs on the charts. He seems very much an excitable boy on the stage, constantly grinning as if in mixed joy and disbelief. Drummer Jim Christie and sax man Erasmo Paolo also lend some musical credence. The last person Roy brings on stage needs no introduction, especially here in Bangor. Stephen King appears and the crowd goes insane. He's a towering six foot two, in a cutoff Maine T-shirt. All eyes are on him, for it is Stephen King, and Stephen King alone, many are here tonight to see.

Then, the Remainders begin to play, and any such singularity promptly disappears. How they did it is a mystery, but it becomes immediately clear: The Rock Bottom Remainders really rock!

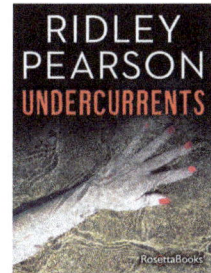

Undercurrents. RosettaBooks 2014

THE MIST

STEPHEN KING
2024 ANNUAL

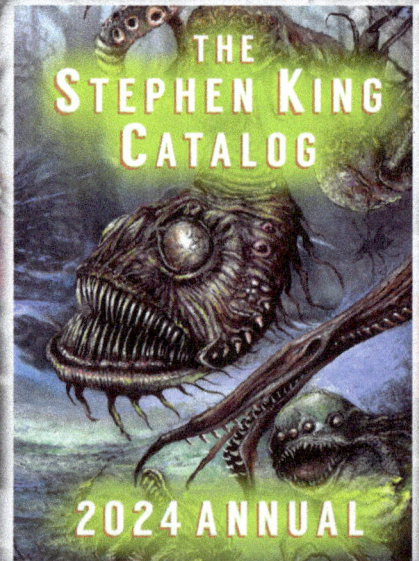

THE STEPHEN KING CATALOG

2024 ANNUAL

Available to order at
StephenKingCatalog.com

Published by
Overlook Connection Press

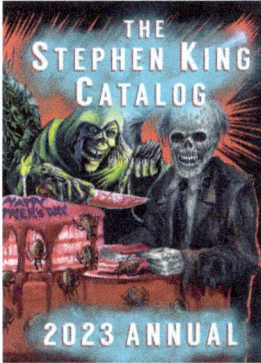

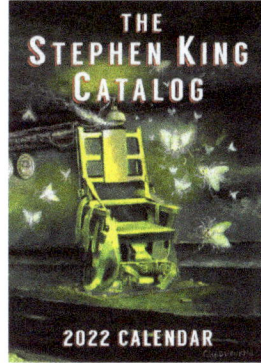

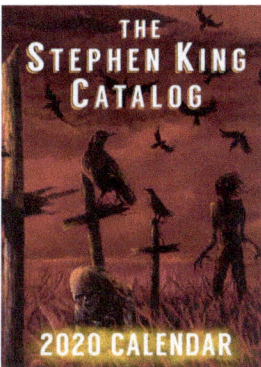

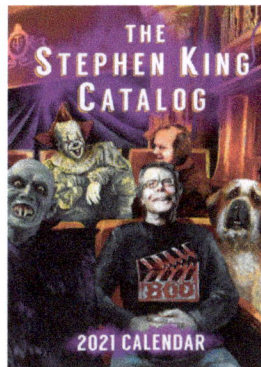

NOVEMBER

17 MONDAY   **18** TUESDAY   **19** WEDNESDAY

The band blasts through the first few numbers, including trademark covers like "Double Shot of My Baby's Love" and "634-5789." The energy in the audience percolates — people have begun dancing wildly in the aisles. Soon, though, for a few brief moments, the stage quiets and we are carried along by the voice of Stephen King, crooning a quite wonderful "Stand by Me." (It truly becomes a rock moment when King breaks into a middle-of-the-song monologue: "I want you to put down that remote control, turn off that TV . . . because you've got two big strong legs . . . and you've got a big, strong man . . . and the only thing I want, except to get laid tonight . . . is for you to stand by me." Cheers follow. This is so cool!)

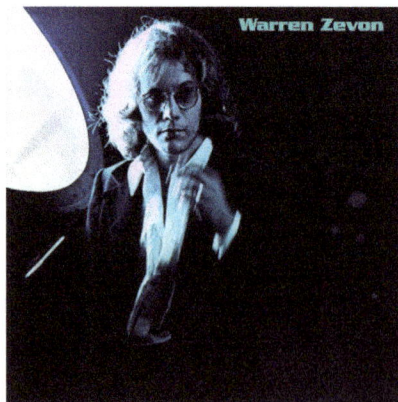

Warren Zevon, 1975

The night is made of such moments: Dave Barry and his wife Michelle Kaufman bouncing through the Micky & Sylvia classic "Love is Strange." Tabitha King, frantically dancing her heart out in the shadows behind the band. Kathi Goldmark taking over center stage with a kickin' "Da Doo Ron Ron." (The Remainderettes are hot!) Dave Marsh, dressed as a dead teenage girl, picketing King's campy, tearful, and fearful rendition of "Teen Angel," as the rest of the band consoles him. (Warren Zevon appears to break into sobs at one point, but I think he was trying to cover up his apoplectic fit of laughter.) Amy Tan's wonderful solos: a weepy "Leader of the Pack," sung to Maine governor Angus King, who sits astride (and subsequently falls from) a Harley in front of the stage; and a Remainders' classic "These Boots are Made for Walkin'," complete with Tan in a severe dominatrix outfit, eventually whipping the boys in the band and calling them all "very, very bad." King's frantic rebel yell of Quiet Riot's 80's version of Slade's original "Cum on Feel the Noize" sent the audience wailing (in a good way.)

NOVEMBER

20 THURSDAY

_____
_____
_____
_____
_____
_____
_____
_____
_____
_____
_____
_____

21 FRIDAY

_____
_____
_____
_____
_____
_____
_____
_____
_____
_____
_____
_____

22 SATURDAY

_____
_____
_____
_____
_____
_____

23 SUNDAY

_____
_____
_____
_____
_____
_____

Dave Barry wrote an original song for this show: "Proofreading Woman," which is hilarious and **actually** a good song (the chorus: "She's got a big dictionary / real good grammar / she never says 'bet**ween** you and I.'")

The show closes with a slam-bang double-shot. The Remainders buzz through the infamous "FBI version" of "Louie Louie" (the only reprintable line is in the chorus, "Get her way down low.") At the end of this, a surprisingly nimble Joel Selvin jumps around the stage in the rapture of a "scream solo" which lasts at least thirty seconds. The finale, King's take on Zevon's famous "Werewolves of London," is terrific fun; if nothing else, the entire night would have been worth it to see Stephen King howl.

The show proper ends and people are getting up from their seats, when a frenzy of light and sound jumps out from the stage. The Remainders retake the room with their encore of Them's "Gloria" (Dave Barry never sounded better). It's one of the truly transcendent moments of the night. You can literally lose yourself in the power of rock and roll.

The Rock Bottom Remainders are not primarily musicians. They are a group of mainly writers **with separate** ideas and agendas, individuals who shape the world individually. But tonight, together, they formed something larger than themselves, something grand, something cohesive.

They were a band, they were magic, and they were sure as hell born to run.

Rock on, Remainders.

– Kevin Quigley

Werewolves of London by Warren Zevon. 1978 by Asylum Records. For radio station use only. Not for sale edition.

NOVEMBER

24 MONDAY

25 TUESDAY

26 WEDNESDAY

THE KING'S GO TO CHURCH

On September 28th, 2017, I was lucky enough to score two tickets to see Stephen King and his son Owen King sit down to speak to their fans about co-authored book *Sleeping Beauties* at the beautiful First Baptist Church in Newton, Massachusetts.

I called my friend Paul, another constant reader, with the good news. As the date approached we we texted each other with our game plan. Paul was going to slide off work a bit early that day with a bit of a sore throat. I took the whole day off to excited to focus on my job. I swung by Paul's house and tooted the horn with three loud blares until he appeared rushing down the front steps to my car.

Photo: Ron Naimo

First Baptist Church, Newton, Massachusetts
On April 15, 1982, it was listed in the
National Register of Historic Places.

I was sporting my *'Salem's Lot* t-shirt. A gift from last Christmas. Paul had on this Red Sox cap and a pretty cool *Creepshow* tee he bought for the occasion. Off we drove and suffered through notorious Boston traffic that late

NOVEMBER

27 THURSDAY
Thanksgiving

_____
_____
_____
_____
_____
_____
_____
_____
_____
_____
_____
_____
_____
_____

28 FRIDAY

_____
_____
_____
_____
_____
_____
_____
_____
_____
_____
_____
_____
_____
_____

29 SATURDAY

_____
_____
_____
_____
_____
_____
_____

30 SUNDAY

_____
_____
_____
_____
_____
_____
_____

Thursday afternoon inching our way along Route 128 towards Newton Centre.
Finally arriving we made our way in and got as close to the altar / stage as we could to get the best view. The stage was lit up and the shiny organ pipes stood out in all their magnificence. As we took a few pictures a familiar face turned to his right. Paul and I knew right away it was actor Chris Cooper! Chris played Al Templeton in the adaption of *11/22/63*. To say we were floored is an understatement. Glad to know even movie stars are fans. Stephen and Owen came out on stage soon after to discuss their co-creative craft and read from their new book.

Actor, Chris Cooper

Photo: Ron Naimo

The price of admission entitled us both to copies of the book and lucky ole me did in fact happen to receive a signed copy, with signatures from both Stephen and Owen. I still have the book and proudly display it on my ever-growing bookshelf with the King family of authors.
I hope maybe to see Stephen and maybe Owen again sometime.
I hope that maybe they will collaborate on a new book together soon.
I hope I never get too old to stop reading their works.
I hope…

— Ron Naimo, Boston

DECEMBER

NO SLEEP 'TIL PARIS

My wife and I visited Paris for 3 days in November 2013 to coincide with Stephen King's visit to MK2 Bibliotheque store, Paris on 13 November 2013 for the *Dr. Sleep* tour.

MK2 Bibliotheque bookstore. Paris, France 2013. Photo: Alan Kyle

We booked a hotel near the venue the day before and visited the store to have a look around. The MK2 Bibliotheque shop was all set up for the King signing the next day.

At dinner we decided it would be a good idea to go

DECEMBER

4 THURSDAY

5 FRIDAY

6 SATURDAY

7 SUNDAY

to the venue early and wait in line. We walked the short distance to the MK2 Bibliotheque around midnight and found many fans already waiting in line. More and more people started to arrive after us and the fans first in line decided to get organized. She gave the first hundred people in line a number corresponding to their place in the line. I was number 89.

It was pretty cold that night and we were finally warmed when the sun came up in the morning. We saw King arriving and the excitement started to build in the line.

While in Germany he was given a Porsche to drive.

The first 100 fans were allowed inside and

Stephen King Arrives in a Porsche
Paris, France 2013 Photo: Alan Kyle

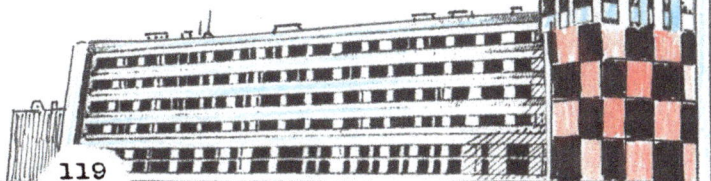

DECEMBER

8 MONDAY

9 TUESDAY

10 WEDNESDAY

Paris, France 2013. Photo: Alan Kyle

the security people informed us that King would only sign one item per person. They were very strict about this as there would be hundreds of fans outside who would not get in.

I decided to chance my luck and put my "The New Lieutenant's Rap" proof inside my *The Shining* UK trade edition to see if he would sign both. When he saw the NLR proof he was excited and he not only signed it, he added a peace sign doodle. I was able to film him signing both. I also

DECEMBER

_____

_____

_____

_____

_____

_____

_____

_____

_____

_____

_____

managed to get him to sign my 'Salem's Lot UK trade edition.

Before we left the store I was able to blag some swag off a French store worker for a few euros. Can't get enough souvenirs. As we left, there was several hundred unfortunate people still waiting in line.

Alan Kyle Photo, Paris, France 2013

After his visit to Paris, King moved on to the US Ramstein Air Base in Rheinland-Pfalz Germany on 18-Nov-23, Zirkus Krone in Munich on 19-Nov-23, and CCH in Hamburg on 20-Nov-23. I was not able to go to any of these events. Next tour!

— Alan Kyle, in France

DECEMBER

15 MONDAY
Hanukkah (1st day)

16 TUESDAY

17 WEDNESDAY

El Rey Theatre, Los Angeles, June 22, 2012

The Rock Bottom Remainders (Official Press Release)
The All-Author Band Announce Their 20th Anniversary & Final
Public Performance During The Past Our Bedtime Tour
In Concert at the El Rey Theatre, Friday, June 22, 2012
LOS ANGELES, CA — May 23, 2012 — The Rock Bottom Remainders, the all-author rock band with Stephen King, Dave Barry, Amy Tan and Matt Groening among its members, will hold their last public concert, after performing together for 20 years, at the El Rey Theatre on Friday, June 22, 2012 at 8:30pm. The show is part of the band's final two-city The Past Our Bedtime Tour, which also includes an appearance not open to the public at the American Library Association Conference in Anaheim on the same weekend. The entire band is together for the first time since 2007. Roger McGuinn, best known as the lead singer and lead guitarist for The Byrds, will also join as a musical guest. Proceeds will benefit literary causes. For more information on the Rock Bottom Remainders, please see www.rockbottomremainders.com.

DECEMBER

18 THURSDAY

_____
_____
_____
_____
_____
_____
_____
_____
_____
_____
_____
_____
_____
_____
_____
_____
_____

19 FRIDAY

_____
_____
_____
_____
_____
_____
_____
_____
_____
_____
_____
_____
_____
_____
_____
_____
_____

20 SATURDAY

_____
_____
_____
_____
_____
_____
_____

21 SUNDAY

_____
_____
_____
_____
_____
_____
_____

Doors open at 7:30pm. Tickets are $40-$200 and go on sale Thursday, May 24, 2012 via TheElRey.com and Ticketmaster. $200 VIP ticket includes pre-show reception and "meet & greet" from 6:30pm to 7:30pm. This is an all-ages show. The historic El Rey Theatre is located in the preserved art deco Miracle Mile district at 5515 Wilshire Blvd., Los Angeles, CA 90036 (323-936-6400). Valet, lot and street parking are available.

> "We play music about as well as Metallica writes novels"
> - Dave Barry

On the upcoming concert, popular horror and science fiction writer Stephen King, who plays rhythm guitar says, "A few years ago, Bruce Springsteen told us we weren't bad, but not to try to get any better otherwise we'd just be another lousy band. After 20 years, we still meet his stringent requirements. For instance, while we all know what 'stringent' means, none of us have yet mastered an F chord."

The Band –

By day, they're authors. Really famous authors. But once a year, they shed their pen-and-pencil clutching personas and become rock stars, complete with roadies, groupies and a wicked cool tour bus. Most of them are both amateur musicians and popular English-language book, magazine, and newspaper authors. Their self-mocking band name was taken from the publishing term "remaindered book," a work of which the unsold remainder of the publisher's stock of copies is sold at a reduced price.

Confirmed for the concert are Stephen King, who hasn't performed with the band since 2007, as well as Amy Tan (vocals & whip), Dave Barry (co-lead guitar),

DECEMBER

22 MONDAY

_____
_____
_____
_____
_____
_____
_____
_____
_____
_____
_____
_____
_____
_____
_____

23 TUESDAY

_____
_____
_____
_____
_____
_____
_____
_____
_____
_____
_____
_____
_____
_____
_____

24 WEDNESDAY
Christmas Eve

_____
_____
_____
_____
_____
_____
_____
_____
_____
_____
_____
_____
_____
_____
_____

Matt Groening (cowbell), Mitch Albom (keyboards), Scott Turow (vocals), James McBride (sax), Greg Iles (co-lead guitar), Ridley Pearson (bass), Roy Blount, Jr. (the crowd), and Sam Barry (harmonica).

King adds, "I'm looking forward to reuniting with all my bandmates. We're older but not dead. Some of us can remember all of the words; all of us can remember some of the words; but NONE of us can remember all of the music. That's why they call it rock and roll."

Barry chimes in, "It's not that we had a 'creative differences' issue, or some in the band wanted to launch solo music careers, but the fact is that we can no longer play an entire set without having to pee." Barry adds, "We realize the Rolling Stones are celebrating 50 years this year, but we don't want to reach the point where our stage moves involve motorized scooters."

1992 May 25th Program booklet,
Cowboy Boogie, Anaheim, CA

Material — The band has two original songs and mostly performs covers. Audiences are likely to be treated to some combination of the following classic tunes performed with The Remainders' unique sensibility, as well as backing up Roger McGuinn on several Byrds classics.

• "Gloria" • "High School Sweater" • "If the House is a Rockin'. . ." • "In the Midnight Hour" • "Louie Louie" • "Paperback Writer" • "Rockaway Beach" • "Stand By Me" Ben E King version • "Steamroller Blues" • "These Boots Are Made for Walkin" • "Wild Thing" • "You Ain't Goin' Nowhere" • "You Can't Judge a Book by its Cover" • "You May Be Right"

Causes — Since the band's founding, they have raised over $2 million for various literacy causes. Proceeds from the Anaheim show support the

DECEMBER

25 THURSDAY
Christmas Eve

26 FRIDAY
Kwanzaa

27 SATURDAY

28 SUNDAY

American Library Association's scholarship program for graduate students in library and information studies. Proceeds from the El Rey show in Los Angeles will benefit The Midnight Mission, the Los Angeles Downtown Women's Center and a new Emerging Author Series at Live Talks Los Angeles to be launched in January 2013. "Kathi founded the Remainders as a one-night stand, and the fling turned us into family who have had 20 years of fun. We promised Kathi she would be on stage with us for our 20th and final year, and so we have. We dedicate these last two shows to our instigator and Remainderette." – Amy Tan

"We play music as well as Metallica writes novels." – Dave Barry

"The Rock Bottom Remainders? Who the hell are they?" – Kirk Hammett, Metallica

DECEMBER

29 MONDAY

30 TUESDAY

31 WEDNESDAY
New Year's Eve

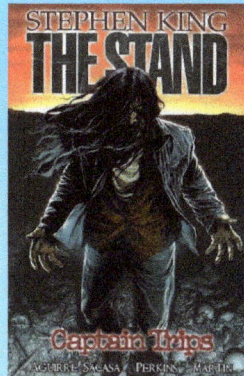

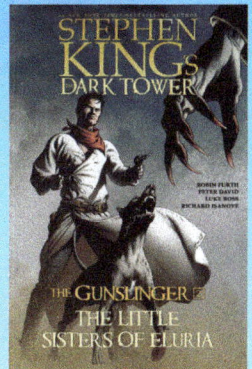

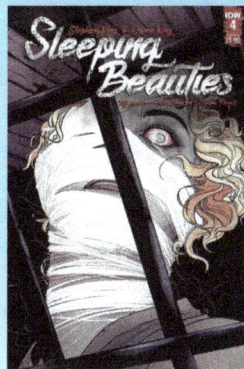

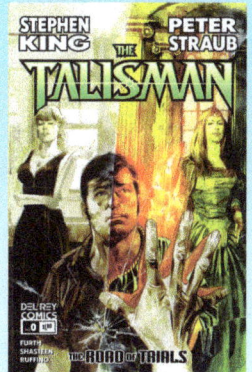

2025 Stephen King Calendar: Meeting Stephen King.
© 2024 by Overlook Connection Press.

"Stars in Their Eyes, Books in Their Arms", "Stephen King Performs at Hank's Place", "Sold More Books Than the Beatles", "A Signing in Jersey", "Vandel…King?", "Hitting Rock Bottom Writing", "King by Candlelight", "Sooner or Later", "My First Stadium Tour!", "Please, Don't Sign the Books" and all text and trivia as noted within the calendar section, ©2024 by Dave Hinchberger.
"'Salem's Lot, 2024 Film Review", ©2024 by Glenn Chadbourne.
"Christine Saves", © 2024 Sean Chard.
"Who's Zoomin' Who?" ©2024 by James Mortimer and Dave Hinchberger.
"Encounters", "Stephen King Drive In" ©2024 by Michael Edwards.
"Six-Pack To Go" ©2024 by Jeffrey Marriotte.
"Film Review: I Know What You Need" ©2024 by Anthony Northrup.
"I Saw Sue Kissing Santa Clause" " ©2024 by Sue Marcus
"Three Kings" ©2024 by T.L. Emery
"Hope Springs Eternal" ©2024 Fran MacBride
"Book Review: The Ideal Genuine Man" ©2024 by Mark Sieber,
"Best Seat in the House" ©2024 by Ed Yarb
"Cujo Meets the Wolves" ©2024 by Noah Mitchell
"Don't Sleep on It" ©2024 by Marie Burns
"The Big Squeeze" ©2024 by Laurie DuPree
"My Life With the Remainders or Why Didn't They Ask Dave Barry?" ©1993, ©2024 by Kathi Kamen Goldmark.
Permissions from Sam Barry.
"Get A Leg Up" ©2024 by Alan Kyle
"Best Birthday Ever ©2024 by Beverly Robinson
"2004 Wannapalooza Tour" ©2004 by Dave Barry, rockbottomremainders.com
"Stephen King Gave Us a Peak Under the Dome" ©2024 by Jason Brenton
"Milk, Bread… Stephen King!… Check!" ©2024 by Cliff Masters
"Rock Bottom Bangor" ©2024 by Kevin Quigley
"The King's Go to Church" ©2024 by Ron Naimo
"No Sleep 'Til Paris" ©2024 by Alan Kyle

Cover, and interior Illustrations © 2024 by Glenn Chadbourne, except where noted.
Layout, design, and border re-creations (of Glenn Chadbourne art) by Bryan McAllister, Fine Dog Creative.

Published © 2024 by Overlook Connection Press. PO Box 1934, Hiram, Georgia 30141
OverlookConnection.com   StephenKingCatalog.com
First Printing   ISBN: 978-1-62330-710-3

VISIT OUR SOCIAL MEDIA to keep up with items posted daily.

stephenkingcatalog   stephenkingcatalog   X @StephenKingCat
stephenkingcatalog   @stephenkingcatalog.bsky.social

BIBLIOGRAPHY, END NOTES, IMAGES

PAGE:8 Email communication with Stephen King @ 2016 Dave Hinchberger

PAGE: 12 Stephen King June 12, 2016 Tweet post.

PAGE: 18-19 2022 Cheltenham Literacy Festival

PAGE: 28-29 "Hitting Rock Bottom", excerpts from On Writing by Stephen King.

PAGE: 35 Photo Earl Hamner on the set of The Waltons in 1976, public domain.

PAGE: 42-43 "Conversation with Stephen King", John F. Kennedy Sixth Floor Museum, Majestic Theatre, Dallas, Texas November 10, 2011. YouTube video.

PAGE: 51 Rock Bottom Remainders photo, rockbottomremainders.com

PAGE: 54-57 Michael Darpino, excerpts from Rock Bottom Remainders Review, April 21, 2010.

PAGE: 76 The Rock Bottom Remainders first press photo, 1993.

PAGE: 88 *Sleeping Beauties* release banner, StephenKing.com, Scribner's cover art 2017.

PAGE: 93 Roger McGuinn, 2004 RockBottomRemainders.com

PAGE: 98-101 Stephen King, Umass 12-7-2012, excerpts and photos, YouTube.com

PAGE: 106-107 William Peter Blatty, wikipedia.com

PAGE: 109 Logo, copyright Tesco

PAGE: 110 Rock Bottom Remainders poster, limited run of 200 copies. Bangor, Maine 1998.

PAGE: 122-125 Rock Bottom Remainders official press release, June 12, 2012.

Glenn Chadbourne art: All calendar border art. 14, 15, 64, 69, 91, 102, 103, 118, 119 copyright 2024

Dave Hinchberger photos: 6, 9, 10, 11, 12 copyright 2016

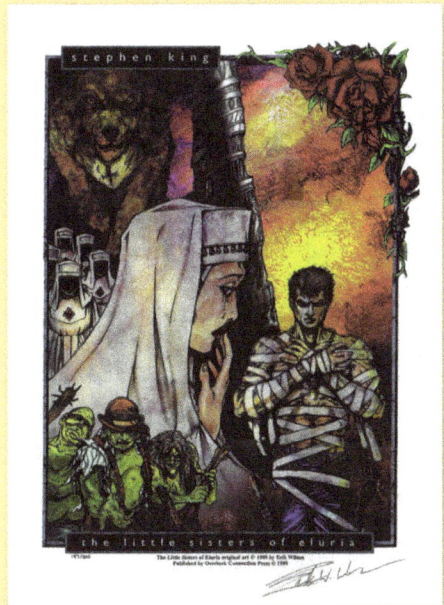

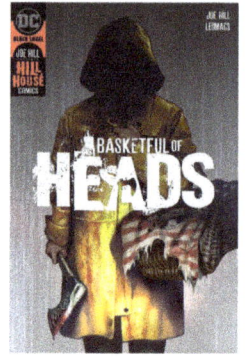
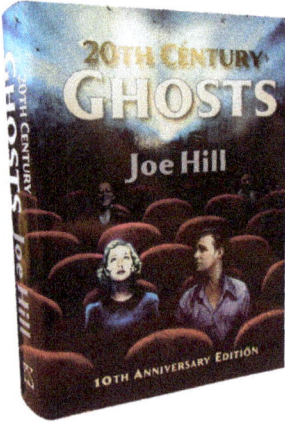
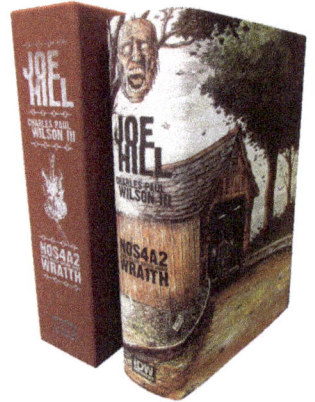
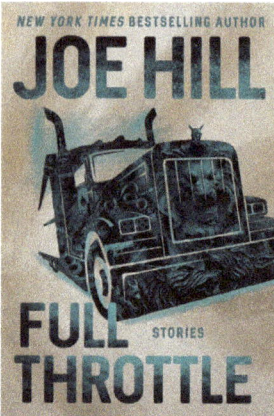

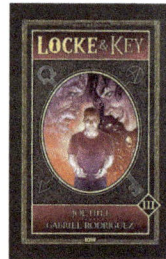
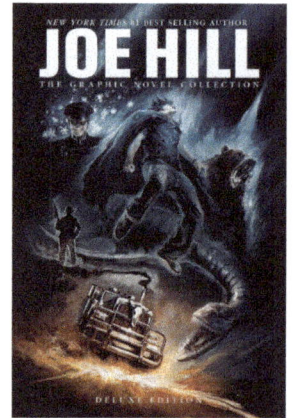
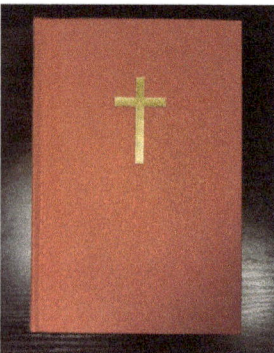